The First-Year Experience
Monograph Series No. 32

PEER LEADERSHIP

A Primer on Program Essentials

Suzanne L. Hamid

Editor

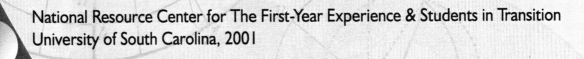

National Resource Center for The First-Year Experience & Students in Transition
University of South Carolina, 2001

Cite as:

      Hamid, S. L. (Ed.). (2001). *Peer leadership: A primer on program essentials* (Monograph No. 32). Columbia, SC: University of South Carolina, National Resource Center for The First-Year Experience and Students in Transition.

Sample chapter citation:

      Hunter, M. S., & Heath M. (2001). The building blocks of the peer leader program: Recruitment, selection, and training. In S. L. Hamid (Ed.), *Peer leadership: A primer on program essentials* (Monograph No. 32) (pp. 37-52). Columbia, SC: University of South Carolina, National Resource Center for The First-Year Experience and Students in Transition.

The Freshman Year Experience® and The First-Year Experience® are service marks of the University of South Carolina. A license may be granted upon written request to use the terms The Freshman Year Experience and The First-Year Experience. This license is not transferrable without written approval of the University of South Carolina.

Additional copies of this monograph may be ordered at $30 each from the National Resource Center for The First-Year Experience and Students in Transition, University of South Carolina, 1629 Pendleton Street, Columbia, SC 29208. Telephone (803) 777-6029. Telefax (803) 777-4699.

Special gratitude is expressed to Tracy L. Skipper, Editorial Projects Coordinator, for editing, design, and layout of this book; to Jean M. Henscheid, Associate Director, for editing; and to Scott Slawinski, Editorial Assistant, for copy editing.

Library of Congress Cataloging-in-Publication Data

Peer leadership : a primer on program essentials / Suzanne Hamid, editor.
      p. cm. — (The first-year experience monograph series ; no. 32)
  Includes bibliographic references.
  ISBN 1-889271-36-5 (alk. paper)
    1. Peer-group tutoring of students—United States. 2. Peer counseling of students—United States. 3. College student orientation—United States. 4. Educational leadership—United States. I. Hamid, Suzanne. II. Series.

LB1031.5 .P46 2001   2001027638
378.1'794—dc21   CIP

Table of Contents

FOREWORD

John N. Gardner

As this monograph on peer leaders comes to print, I must admit that I feel like a parent who was present at the conception (in this case of the monograph) but who didn't show up again until the delivery, providing no input during the first nine months of development. Nevertheless, I take some ownership of the original inspiration for the project, based on my recognition of a lack of literature on this topic, particularly as it related to the role of peer leaders in first-year seminars. This recognition of gaps in scholarly literature and attempts to fill those gaps are the basic and historic mission of the National Resource Center for The First-Year Experience and Students in Transition. This monograph now joins a long tradition of more than 30 other publications designed to do exactly that. Two short decades ago there essentially was no literature on the topic of what has become known as The First-Year Experience; now we are finally addressing this very significant deficiency in describing the work of a cohort of individuals who are extremely influential in shaping that first-year experience, namely, our peer leaders.

While this monograph explores the contributions of a variety of peer leaders, I believe those in first-year seminars offer a solid test case from which others may learn. My focus, therefore, rests primarily on them.

I begin by looking back on my quarter century directing the first-year seminar at the University of South Carolina, during which time I witnessed a handful of momentous changes to our University 101 course. In retrospect, I believe these have been the most significant:

1. Building in ongoing assessment from an independent and institution-wide perspective

2. Converting the original pass/fail grading to letter grading

3. Adopting a parallel or bookend course—the senior capstone course, University 401, at the University of South Carolina—to the first-year seminar

4. Developing a new faculty/staff orientation program based on a set of assumptions similar to those used in the design of the original first-year seminar

5. Introducing the peer leader concept to the first-year seminar course

Of course I did not arrive at the peer leader concept alone; I acknowledge my indebtedness to three institutions where I saw this concept thriving long before I ever introduced it at the University of South Carolina. Specifically, I was inspired by and finally decided to emulate the peer leader programs I saw in place at my alma mater, Marietta College, at Baldwin-Wallace College, and at Kean University in New Jersey. On all three of these very different campuses, a vibrant partnership existed among faculty, academic administrators, and student affairs officers—a partnership dedicated to the functional integration of highly motivated and well-trained undergraduate student leaders into programs designed to orient new students to college and to ensure the success of those same students. Having seen these three powerful illustrations, in the Fall of 1993, I enlisted the aid of one of my former first-year seminar students, Ms. Lisa Huttinger. Together, we designed a syllabus and team taught a first-year seminar for approximately 20 students. I was so impressed with her contributions to the development of her fellow students and to the positive impact of this role on her in terms of her communication skills, self-esteem, and confidence, that I suggested we adopt this model throughout the University 101 course. Dan Berman, now Director of University 101 at the University of South Carolina, developed and implemented the peer leader program as we know it today at USC. As Mary Stuart Hunter and Misty Heath illustrate in Chapter 4, the University 101 peer leader program continues to thrive with nearly 100 peer leaders poised to serve in instructional roles in Fall 2001.

Despite its current success, the peer leader program did meet with some initial resistance. In particular, we were greeted with two unique arguments for not using peer leaders when we attempted to launch and expand the program at the University of South Carolina. These are worth sharing. One basis for opposition was the perception on the part of potential instructors that student partners essentially would be "spies of the administration," or at the very least for the faculty program leadership. While this was certainly never our intent, it has indeed been an unintended consequence. For example, peer leaders sometimes become so invested in the success of their student charges that they report to program administrators instructional partners who are, in their opinion, performing at less than ideal levels or who take excess liberties with respect to absenting themselves from class, etc. Another strongly voiced objection to assigning peer leaders to work with instructors was the perception that in using peers, the instructors would experience greater demands on their time than if they had taught a course without a peer leader. This is a potentially valid concern that needs to be further explored and evaluated; I know of no empirical evidence to support this notion one way or the other. Most likely, it does take more time for an instructor to work with a peer in some facets of the first-year seminar, for example, in syllabus planning. On the other hand, peers can and do save instructors valuable time in such areas as making arrangements for class activities and in following up with students outside of class.

In addition to overcoming these sources of resistance, one of the most important decisions we at the University of South Carolina had to make when launching the program in the first place was determining the criteria for selection of peer leaders. The other authors in this monograph and I are not here to argue that readers ought to follow the model of the University of South Carolina, of Lee University, of Kean University, or of any of the other programs profiled here. But, in this one area, I wish to share my bias. I believe this particular kind of instruction is best served by setting the highest academic standards for the selection of the peer leaders. As higher educators, we must model in the selection of these peer instructors the idea that one can be both academically and socially successful in the undergraduate collegiate environment. It is not sufficient for peers merely to demonstrate a high degree of extroversion on the Myers Briggs Type Indicator and a solid C average. Instead, I see the peer leader concept as an opportunity not only for the most academically able students to lead their peers but also as an opportunity for the institution to make a further investment in the education of its most outstanding students.

Admittedly, this may strike some readers as a rather elitist posture, and I wish to acknowledge that. However, these kinds of students are those who, in many cases, will reflect most favorably on our institutions in the future. In return for the future benefits they will provide to our institutions, I strongly believe they deserve this additional academic development experience. In fact, my experience with the peer leader concept has led me to conclude that the most important impact of the University 101 program, in particular, and of the first-year seminar concept, in general, may well be on the peer leaders who serve as co-teachers rather than on the first-year students they serve. This is a contention, however, which still needs to be borne out in future research. I am grateful to the authors of this monograph for exploring this and a variety of other administrative issues related to peer leader programs.

Aside from the benefits to the peers themselves and the students they serve, why should institutions adopt peer leader programs? Perhaps one of the most important reasons for launching a peer leader program is to leverage the institution's chances of influencing student behaviors and attitudes in those directions in which it would like to see students move, particularly in those ways that might be consistent with the institutional mission. There is enormous empirical evidence in the higher education literature to suggest that the most significant, influential variable on stu-

dent growth and change during the college years is the influence of other students. Therefore, it is axiomatic to the authors that one of the best ways to influence students is through other students.

The power of the peer leader concept is also related to the change agent role that first-year seminars have come to play on many campuses. These venues have, in effect, become experimental incubators to test out and legitimize pedagogical strategies and partnerships that are less likely to be attempted in higher status areas of the curriculum. A manifestation of this important role of the first-year seminars is the hope of many course directors that the successful use of peer leaders in the first-year seminar will spur the adoption of the concept in other instructional settings. In her introduction to the monograph, Suzanne Hamid provides an example of this expansion at her own institution, Lee University, where two academic departments in addition to the first-year seminar program are now using peer leaders and where peers are also used in the academic advising program.

Finally, I believe, and lament, that we higher educators often are not nearly intentional enough about recruiting our successors. How often do we fail to reach out to our very best students, to ask them to consider the possibility of joining our profession after college, especially as college teachers? I see the peer leader program as a potential vehicle for introducing students, while in college, to the excitement and intrinsic gratification inherent in college teaching. We must remember that very few entering undergraduates have ever had any prior contact with college professors, let alone student affairs professionals, and hence it is unlikely that they would have given any consideration to becoming a higher educator. The peer leader concept seems to me to be one of the most powerful ways of addressing this deficiency. By engaging students in meaningful partnerships with faculty and administrators, we provide them with valuable insight into our work and ensure a legacy of academic success for future generations of students.

I congratulate the many educators who have implemented this concept on their campuses and thank them for the many valuable lessons they have provided. I hope the readers of this monograph will find here the tools they need to guide their planning and practice as they design and expand peer leader programs on their own campuses.

University of South Carolina
February, 2001

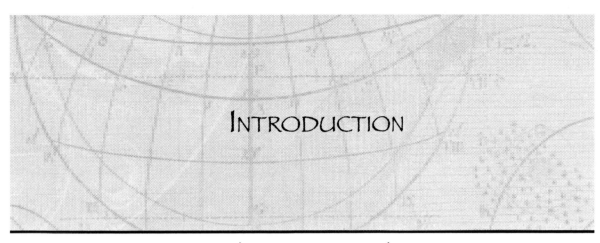

INTRODUCTION

Suzanne L. Hamid

Five years ago, while attending a Freshman Year Experience conference, I was present at a session on the topic of peer leadership in the first-year seminar course. Not being familiar with the concept, I was curious about the principle behind it. My professional work had long revolved around creating successful transitions for students, and I also had a genuine interest in fostering the leadership skills of talented students. I was struck by what appeared to be an overwhelmingly positive situation for all groups associated with the endeavor. From the account I heard, this type of program was providing an excellent leadership opportunity for many outstanding upperclass students, a support system for the students they served, and an array of benefits for the institution as a whole. I listened, intrigued, as peer leaders from the University of South Carolina told their stories, and I recognized peer leadership programs as unique and promising vehicles for merging my twin goals of creating successful transitions and providing meaningful leadership opportunities.

The following year, my institution, Lee University, piloted a peer leader program with four upperclass students. This experiment proved successful in several respects and resulted in the creation of a full-fledged peer leader program to enhance our then-disdained first-year seminar course. Since the inception of the peer leader program, the first-year seminar *Gateway* program is stronger than ever, and Lee University's peer leaders appear to have had a tremendous impact on first-year students, as reflected in the 7% increase in retention of first-year students. Two other academic departments within the institution have since incorporated peer leaders in their efforts to improve teaching and learning, and a peer advising program is now a successful component of the institution's academic advising system. Ours is not an isolated story. Higher education researchers continue to provide us with evidence that the most significant impact on learning and adjustment within the college experience stems from the influence of students on other students. How to harness this influence through peer leadership programs is the topic of this monograph.

One of our early dilemmas in conceptualizing this publication was the question of how broadly we were going to define the use of peer leadership in higher education. In the opening chapter, Steven Ender and Keaghan Kay present various descriptors for peer leadership on college campuses, including the terms *peer educator, peer helper, student paraprofessional*, and *student assistant*. They cite the following definition for these roles: "Paraprofessionals are students who have been selected and trained to offer educational services to their peers. These services are intentionally designed to assist in the adjustment, satisfaction, and persistence of students toward attainment of their educational goals" (qtd. in Ender & Kay, p. 1). Whereas Ender and Kay focus on a broad range of paraprofessional experiences, the majority of examples and practices in this publication are taken from the use of undergraduate students who serve as co-teachers in first-year seminar courses. This choice allows the authors to draw from the scholarship and practical experiences they know best. While the term "peer instructor" may more aptly describe the work of these students, we have chosen to use the more generic "peer leader" throughout the monograph. This decision was based primarily on data collected from the 1997 National Survey on First-Year Seminar Programs conducted by the National Resource Center for The First-Year Experience and Students in Transition. In this survey, most institutions reported using the term "peer leaders" to identify students who assist in first-year seminar courses.

We are confident that readers whose work with paraprofessionals is not in first-year seminar courses will still find these and other examples helpful. We believe many of the practices illustrated in this monograph, both within and beyond the classroom, are generic enough to be relevant to a wide range of peer leadership programs. Moreover, many of the lessons highlighted here relate to all types of peer leadership initiatives. The following chapters will offer readers the theoretical principles behind the practice of peer leadership and will showcase a collection of programs and perspectives that demonstrate how peer leadership is being practiced at institutions of higher learning across the U.S. Further, this monograph will emphasize the essentials of a well-coordinated program, including building blocks of implementation, components of administration, and the impact of peer leadership on various student populations at several institutions, including the impact on peer leaders themselves.

This monograph is a blend of the theoretical and the practical and is written by practitioners and scholars in the field who have invested more than 100 years of combined service toward the advocacy of students helping students. The work they perform on their individual campuses along with their areas of specialization have helped to shape the content, direction, and tone of this publication. In working on this monograph, the authors discovered that although many institutions of higher learning espouse the value of students helping students, the topic of how to design and administer peer leadership programs is a relatively minor one in higher education's contemporary literature. The literature that does exist generally provides a rationale for peer leadership or serves as a textbook for the peer leaders themselves. This prompts our emphasis in this publication on program essentials designed to help those who are considering a peer leader program or seeking to improve an existing one.

As described earlier, Chapter 1 affirms the deep historical roots of peer leadership in higher education. In addition to defining the peer leadership role, Steven Ender and Keaghan Kay provide theoretical support for this concept with a thorough literature review. In addition to providing a theoretical basis for peer leadership programs, Ender and Kay trace the past 40 years of peer leadership on American college campuses. Further, they present information from several studies pertaining to this subject, including a discussion on the value of maximizing program outcomes when planning and administering peer leadership programs.

Chapter 2 contextualizes the work of peer leaders by offering a general discussion of leadership education. Here, Vicky Orazem and Ashley Roller begin with the historical development of leadership theory and highlight some of the characteristics contemporary theorists suggest are necessary for effective leadership development. They conclude by describing leadership models from five institutions to support their premise that a new kind of leader is developing among students serving as peer leaders.

In Chapter 3, Christopher Lynch provides a primer on the essentials of implementing a successful peer leader program. Drawing on his own experience and on examples from several institutions, Lynch argues that the success of the peer leader-faculty relationship is dependent on a variety of issues surrounding accountability, organization, and administration of peer leader programs. He highlights fundamental communication skills and strategies, basic attitudes, and practices that can foster a "low maintenance" peer leader program.

Chapter 4 explores three of the building blocks essential to the success of any peer leader program—*recruitment, selection, and training*. Mary Stuart Hunter and Misty Heath examine a cluster of factors, standards, and techniques associated with these three essentials. Using practical, concrete examples, these authors supply novice and experienced program facilitators a blueprint of the *who, what, why, when,* and *where* of peer leader recruitment, selection, and training.

As indicated earlier, a significant portion of this monograph is devoted to the use of peer leaders in first-year seminar courses. However, Chapter 5 explores a variety of other roles peer leaders often assume on campus. Here, Marmy Clason and John Beck report on peer leader work designed to enhance both the academic and social experiences of students. They showcase specific programs and practices from a variety of institutions across the U.S., including those in the two-year sector, to demonstrate how peer leaders are making a difference in areas beyond the classroom.

The World Wide Web and other new technologies have been hailed as catalysts ushering in a new era for education. In Chapter 6, Jean Henscheid and Gary Brown forecast a change in the role of peer leaders brought by new educational delivery methods. The authors emphasize the efforts of educators to integrate two pedagogical approaches: peer education and new technologies. Readers are introduced to an exemplary institutional model for coupling peer leadership and interactive and generative computer-enriched learning and are offered implementation strategies and general recommendations.

In Chapter 7, Jayson VanHook and I review data collected in 1999 on 40 peer leader programs attached to first-year seminar programs. Profiles of institutions, peer leader programs, and peer leaders are presented. The chapter highlights four peer leader programs and their correlation with increased student satisfaction, enhanced learning, and higher rates of retention. Readers are also provided with anecdotal evidence of benefits to peer leaders.

In Chapter 8, John Gardner and I offer a summary of the major ideas in the monograph and present specific recommendations based on those ideas. We offer readers implications for the future of peer leadership and outline specific directions for campus policy makers and other leaders regarding the use of undergraduate students as peer leaders.

This publication would not have come to fruition without the vision, ideas, and shared interest of many wonderful individuals. Their contributions toward this project, from its conception to conclusion, were invaluable! First, I thank John Gardner for conceiving the idea for this monograph and for giving me this opportunity. Jean Henscheid and Tracy Skipper of the National Resource Center for The First-Year Experience and Students in Transition deserve much credit for their editorial assistance, ideas, and support. The chapter authors are to be commended for their work, which represents some of the best thinking in this field. Their timeliness and graciousness of manner and spirit throughout this entire period are greatly appreciated. All of us involved in this monograph hope it will assist and inform you as you explore the use of peer leaders as a vehicle for advancing the efforts of higher education.

Lee University
December, 2000

CHAPTER 1

PEER LEADERSHIP PROGRAMS: A RATIONALE AND REVIEW OF THE LITERATURE

Steven C. Ender and Keaghan Kay

This chapter focuses on the positive benefits of students serving in leadership and helping roles on college campuses. A review of the literature on peer influence is presented along with several studies that have documented the extensive use of students in helping roles for the past 40 years. A definition of peer leadership is provided along with several recommendations educators may consider in order to strengthen the planning process of peer leadership programs.

For purposes of this chapter, the term peer leadership is used interchangeably with other descriptors of students helping students on college campuses. These terms include peer educator, peer helper, student paraprofessional, student assistant, student aid, and student helper. The term used to describe this helping role is not as important as a description of what students do (or do not do) in the role. This chapter uses the definition of peer leaders provided by Ender (1984) as he describes the role of students helping students in campus paraprofessional roles:

> Paraprofessionals are students who have been selected and trained to offer educational services to their peers. These services are intentionally designed to assist in the adjustment, satisfaction, and persistence of students toward attainment of their educational goals. Students performing in paraprofessional roles are compensated for their services and supervised by qualified professionals. (p. 324)

Expanding on this definition to provide a context for campus services, Ender (1984) emphasizes that students serving in helping roles are providing assistance to others that promotes student adjustment, satisfaction, and persistence. These services are provided through various interventions including assisting, coaching, problem solving, encouraging, modeling, and supporting, rather than functions such as remediating, training, counseling, or interpreting. These latter functions are reserved for the student leader's professional counterpart. These are important distinctions to consider as one plans and implements a peer leadership program.

Peer leaders support students as they explore, identify, and apply problem-solving strategies to resolve everyday problems and challenges that occur in the student maturation process (Ender & Newton, 2000). Intervention programs staffed by undergraduate leaders are designed with special attention to these intended outcomes.

Peer Influence

No discussion or consideration regarding the uses of students in helping roles can take place without some understanding of the significance theorists and educational researchers attribute to the effects of peer influence. The literature of the last four decades clearly suggests that students can have a significant positive impact on the growth and development of other students. Several researchers and authors of significant position papers within the higher education community have emphasized the peer group's positive effect on student development.

For example, the report of the Committee on the Student in Higher Education (The Hazen Report, 1968), written to help the higher education community gain an understanding of how various social and psychological influences shape student attitudes, interests, and activities, pays special attention to the effects of the peer group. The report states, "Just as the friendship group controls production on a factory assembly line and cohesiveness in a military squad, so the student friendship group helps determine what is learned in the college, how it is learned, and what effect both knowledge and the learning experience have on the student's total personality" (p. 13). This report also indicates that the most effective teachers on a college campus are usually other students, a fact that drives the success of many peer educator programs. The Hazen Report acknowledged that, in 1968, the research data supporting the positive contributions students could make to others in the educational process was meager. However, the authors believed the influence was so obvious that higher educa-

> . . . the most effective teachers on a college campus are usually other students, a fact that drives the success of many peer educator programs.

tion should proceed rapidly to understand how it works.

During that same time period, other researchers began to investigate the impact of peers on other students and their results substantiated the Hazen Report's assertion. For example, Heath (1968), in his significant research in the area of student maturation and variables that affect the maturation process, asserts that "educators tend to ignore the powerful maturing effects that a young person's personal friendships may have" (p. 5). Heath's research also concludes that one powerful influence on student maturation is the student's interpersonal relationships with other students.

Arthur Chickering, a second researcher working in the field of student development at that time, was also studying variables that affect college student growth. Among the many conclusions of his research, Chickering (1969) agrees that the peer group is a powerful influence on student development. He states that "relationships with close friends and peer groups, or sub-cultures, are primary forces influencing student development in college" (Chickering, 1969, p. 253).

In 1972, Robert D. Brown, writing *Student Development in Tomorrow's Higher Education—A Return to the Academy*, added further insight regarding the powerful impact students could have on other students while in college. He states, "one of the most potent environmental influences on student development in college is the peer group" (p. 31). Brown asserts that students influence each other most in changing social attitudes and personality. He goes on to argue that "socialization, as much as information, is likely to have an impact on attitudes toward grades, future aspirations, and life goals" (p. 31). Also, he reminds us that "faculty influence on student attitudes and values is relatively limited when compared to the power of the peer group" (p. 31).

More recent research supports and expands upon these earlier findings. Pascarella and Terenzini (1991), in their review of major findings regarding how college affects students, comment that

> ... students' interactions with their peers also have a strong influence on many aspects of change during college. Included are such areas as intellectual development and orientation; political, social, and religious values; academic and social self-concept; intellectual orientation; interpersonal skills; moral development; general maturity and personal development; and educational aspirations and educational attainment. (pp. 620-621)

One persistent theme regarding the effects of college on students emerges from the work of Pascarella and Terenzini and is of critical importance when considering the use of student leaders. According to the authors, this theme reveals "the central role of other people in a student's life, whether students or faculty, and the character of the learning environments they create and the nature and strength of the stimulation their interactions provide for learning and change of all kinds" (1991, p. 648). They urge faculty and administrators to shape the educational and interpersonal experiences and settings of their campus in ways that will promote learning and achievement of the institution's educational goals and to induce students to become involved in those activities, to exploit those settings and opportunities to the fullest.

For those responsible for designing and implementing peer leadership programs, this goal should be in the forefront of their thinking. In fact, Pascarella and Terenzini (1991) specifically discuss the importance of orientation and continuing orientation programs for new students to stimulate earlier and more enduring involvement in the academic and social systems of an institution. Further, they suggest, "it is also reasonable to expect that student in-

volvement will be greatest if new students can be immediately linked with people who are already invested in the institution, whether faculty members or other students" (p. 650). These researchers have provided solid evidence for campus administrators and faculty to create intentionally designed peer leadership programs focusing on the first-year experience of college students.

Joseph Cuseo (1991) reports that peers have the capacity to "elicit the involvement" of first-year students more effectively than professional staff or faculty members because they "are not perceived as intimidating authority figures" (p. 9). Regarding peer advising, Derell Hart (1995) suggests peer leader programs may help overcome some of the barriers facing traditional advising and support programs:

> peer-assisted or peer-delivered reach-out advising information programs should be viewed as opportunities to increase the visibility, utilization, and effectiveness of academic advising services for students. These types of programs provide students with academic information in readily accessible formats and provide both a way to respond to the problem of students failing to seek and obtain valuable academic information… and a means to expand the amount and quality of advising services available to entering students. (p. 81)

Terenzini, Pascarella, and Blimling (1996) provide other support regarding the positive effects of peer interaction. Through a review of the literature related to how students' out-of-class experiences influence learning and cognitive development, they conclude that the peer group can play a significant and positive role. Terenzini et. al (1996) conclude: When peer interactions involve educational or intellectual activities or topics, the effects are almost always beneficial to students; and discussing racial/ethnic issues in student-peer interactions appears to contribute to students' overall academic development and to gains in general knowledge, critical thinking, and analytical and problem-solving skills. These findings have specific implications for much of the work performed by student leaders working in residence halls, tutoring and study skills centers, and programs emphasizing cross-cultural understanding and communication.

No review of peer group effects is complete without some attention to the findings of Astin's (1993) research published in *What Matters in College*. Exploring how students change and develop and determining how colleges can enhance the developmental process, Astin (1993) concludes: "the student's peer group is the single most potent source of influence on growth and development during the undergraduate years...students' values, beliefs, and aspirations tend to change in the direction of the dominant values, beliefs, and aspirations of the peer group" (p. 398).

Of special importance to those who implement peer leadership programs is Astin's (1993) explanation of how the peer group facilitates learning and personal development. Astin explains the impact of this positive effect from two perspectives: the individual (or psychological) point of view and the group (or sociological) point of view.

Individual Point of View

The individual perceives his or her peer group as a collection of individuals with whom he/ she wishes to identify and to affiliate and seeks this group's acceptance and approval. Astin (1993) uses the term identification to refer to a person's belief "that I am like these other people in certain key respects and that they are like me" (p. 400). In the context of peer leadership, the student serving in the helping role is a model of the affiliation peer group and has the skills to assist others to become more like the group. Some examples include students who have made the adjustment to campus life (e.g., peer leaders working in ongoing orientation), students who have mastered a

difficult subject (e.g., tutors and Supplemental Instruction leaders), and students who live successfully in campus residence halls (e.g., resident assistants). Peer leaders serving in these roles can assist other college students to become more like the individuals with whom they wish to identify.

Group Point of View

For the purpose of describing the peer effect on an individual, Astin (1993) defines the peer group as "any group of individuals in which the members identify, affiliate with, and seek acceptance and approval from *each other*" (p. 401). From this perspective, it is important for the student to have the desire to seek acceptance and approval from the group. According to Astin, the norms and expectations of the group's members promote this desire. For example, the student struggling to feel "at home" on the college campus is affected by the group norm that most students do adjust in a matter of weeks or months. In most classes, the group norm is the successful accomplishment of course objectives; and in the residence hall, most students on the floor learn to live with and adjust to one another. Those not meeting the expectations of the larger group in all three areas will typically experience negative reinforcement from the larger, dominant group. Peer leaders in helping roles can assist students in all three examples to discover strategies to gain acceptance and approval from the larger group.

Use of Peers in Leadership Roles

While researchers have demonstrated the many positive benefits of peer interaction, practitioners have made wide use of undergraduates in helping and supporting campus roles over the years. At least six major national studies have been conducted since 1959 investigating the use of undergraduates in helping roles (Powell, 1959; Brown & Zunker, 1966; Zunker, 1975; Salovey, 1983; Ender & Winston, 1984; Ender, 1984; Winston & Ender, 1988; and

Carns, Carns, & Wright, 1993). Several notable trends can be identified through a review of these studies. First, the number of institutions reporting the use of students in leadership roles has increased since the first study in 1959. Leadership roles for students appear to have increased, rising from 67% of responding institutions in 1959 to 83% in the 1993 study. The use of peer leaders has grown steadily, generally moving upward throughout the entire period from 67% (Powell, 1959), 66% (Brown & Zunker, 1966), 76% (Zunker, 1975), 78% (Salovey, 1983), and 72% (Ender & Winston, 1984) to 83% (Carns, Carns, & Wright, 1993).

Second, the number of campus settings and services using student helpers has increased substantially. In the first study by Powell (1959), students were employed primarily in new student orientation and residence hall work. By 1984, use was found to have increased across a number of program settings (Ender, 1984). Beyond student orientation (82%) and residence halls (81%), students were found to be used in leadership positions in student judiciary programs (55%), student activities (54%), counseling (34%), placement centers (33%), religious centers (20%), advising programs (33%), study skills (18%), and crises intervention (20%). Carns, Carns, and Wright (1993) validate this expanded use of student helpers through their national survey demonstrating a 96% use in residence life, 39% use in academic departments, 73% use in reading/study habits centers, 30% use in student social centers, and 22% in student religious centers. These authors also note that undergraduate students participate in new student orientation at 91% of responding institutions.

A third observation of these studies suggests that student leaders are being used in group intervention more than in individual intervention (Carns, Carns, & Wright, 1993), with the greatest increases in the use of group intervention occurring in both reading study habits and educational program planning areas.

Obviously, faculty and administrators have recognized the powerful positive educational impact of placing students in campus leadership positions to assist their peers. The growth in the popularity of this intervention in the past 45 years has been significant with institutions incorporating peer helping into a variety of their services. As we know from the literature and research, peers affect peers. We also have substantial documentation that colleges and universities are attempting to capitalize on this fact through programs staffed by peer leaders. But what do we know about the effectiveness of peer leaders?

Effectiveness in Leadership Roles

The effectiveness of peer leaders has been demonstrated repeatedly in the literature. In the 1960s and 70s, many researchers (Carkhuff, 1968; Delworth, Sherwood, & Casaburri, 1974; Carkhuff & Truax, 1965; and Zunker & Brown, 1966) concluded that paraprofessional counselors could be as effective or only slightly less effective than professional staff members in providing general counseling and academic adjustment counseling to others. Brown and Myers (1975) found that students who had received academic advising from other students had more positive attitudes toward their advisors and lower dropout rates than students advised solely by faculty. When comparing the effectiveness of student-trained paraprofessionals with that of professionals in leading social anxiety management groups, Barrow and Hetherington (1981) found that subjects in both groups improved significantly. When Ender and Winston (1984) asked professionals to provide a rationale for implementing paraprofessional student-staffed

> Peer leaders in helping roles can assist students. . . to discover strategies to gain acceptance and approval from the larger group.

programs, more than half of the respondents said that students could be more effective than professionals in assisting other students with their normal developmental concerns.

Carns, Carns, and Wright (1993) cite several studies (Brenden, 1986; Frisz & Lane, 1987; Kramer & Hardy, 1985; and Russell & Skinkle, 1990) that demonstrate the specific, positive outcomes of students serving their peer group through the interventions of peer advisement and peer counseling. These authors also cite studies (Berg & Wright-Buckley, 1988; Lewis, 1986; and Locke & Zimmerman, 1987) that show the effectiveness of peer counseling to assist in the adjustment of minority students to campus. Jones, Barnes, and Tryon-Baker (1990) report positive results using peer education programs in the areas of acquaintance rape, HIV/AIDS, healthy relationships, and stress management on a two-year campus.

Other studies point directly to the effectiveness of peer-led programs designed to compliment the first-year experience. A study reported by Rabiecki and Brabeck (1985), investigating a program designed to meet first-year student adjustment needs, concludes that although faculty were most helpful in general academic and career-related issues, peer advisers were most helpful with social and adjustment issues. In examining extended orientation programs, Ragle and Krone (1985) demonstrate that peer telephone contact with first-year students after they had matriculated was perceived as an effective method not only for delivering information and making referrals but also for personalizing a large university environment.

Planning to Maximize Program Outcomes

In order to gain full advantage of the powerful impact of peer interaction, program administrators must carefully determine the outcomes they are seeking as they plan their peer leadership program. These outcomes drive all other important program variables, including

selection of student leaders, training, and ongoing supervision.

The ultimate success or failure of peer leadership programs lies, in part, in effective and thoughtful planning in regard to program outcomes. Questions to be asked at this early planning stage include: (a) How do we select and train peer leaders? (b) How will students be different as a result of interacting with student leaders (i.e., what will they learn)? (c) How many students do we wish to serve in any given academic term through this intervention? (d) What evidence do we have that the intervention is needed, and what evidence do we need to collect to determine that the need has been met? and (e) What values of the institution have we reinforced through the peer leadership program?

Program planners who spend time answering these five questions prior to implementing their program will find that the answers guide all subsequent program implementation decisions. A discussion of the five questions concludes this chapter.

How Do We Select and Train Peer Leaders?

Selection. As we have learned, the positive effect peers have on one another occurs partially through a student's desire to be more like and to affiliate with other members of the dominant group. Therefore, we should consider students who are successful in the dominant group as potential peer leaders. Defining a concept of success is critical to this process. For example, how do we describe a student who has successfully adjusted to our campus, our academic expectations, and our residence halls? This description leads to the identification of potential peer leaders—students who consistently model the behaviors and knowledge we identify as successful. Mullendore and Abraham (1993) suggest establishing basic guidelines, including determining what qualities a student leader should possess, developing a selection procedure that will help identify these qualities, implementing the selection process, and conducting an evaluation of the selection process to determine effectiveness. Researchers agree that efforts must be made to encourage diversity (Mullendore & Abraham, 1993). In their work on paraprofessional staffing, McDaniels, Carter, Heinzen, Candrl, and Weiberg (1994) advocate finding a "good cross-section" by establishing criteria based on ethnicity, gender, major, living environment, year in school, skills, and leadership experience. They also recommend hiring students who will represent the office or center for as long as possible, thus selecting students who are not beyond the second semester of their junior year. In addition, McDaniels et al. (1994) suggest screening candidates for minimum qualifications, such as GPA and undergraduate status. Faculty can recommend peer leaders; former or current peer leaders can help recruit new members; information booths/table tents might be set up in residence halls or cafeterias (the authors state that this method is most effective with first-year students and sophomores); welcome tours and student newspapers can be used to recruit new peer leaders. Mullendore and Abraham (1993) insist that information meetings are also necessary to ensure that students have a clear understanding of the selection/interview process and what will be expected of them in their position as peer leaders. Readers are encouraged to consult Carns, Carns, and Wright (1993) for research regarding selection procedures used in peer leadership programs.

Training. Since student leaders are the ones "in the trenches," it is critical that they are trained properly (Mullendore & Abraham, 1993, p. 70). Mullendore and Abraham (1993) offer the following basic guidelines to consider while developing a training program: (a) assess training needs of student leaders, (b) design appropriate training program based on these needs, (c) conduct training, and (d) evaluate training. In the peer leader-

ship role, modeling is critical; however, having a skill and helping another to acquire this same skill typically requires training for the peer leader.

Again, knowing the outcomes of the planned intervention will begin to shape the skills that must be transmitted in training. Will the peer leader work with individuals or groups (or both) when performing his or her role? Will the desired outcome(s) require coaching, mentoring, problem solving, or telling? All of these questions have implications for training content and duration. Mullendore and Abraham (1993) note that the overarching desired outcome is for students to have good communication skills, understand the services the institution offers, make appropriate referrals, and come together as a team. McDaniels et al. (1994) stress the

> The ultimate success or failure of peer leadership programs lies, in part, in effective and thoughtful planning in regard to program outcomes.

team-oriented approach "in which the paraprofessionals are empowered by their supervisors as mentors, confidants, and role models. In turn, the supervisors take on a higher level of responsibility which requires them to develop their own style of management and learn how to be effective role models" (p. 106).

Some institutions offer training as semester-long, for-credit courses that emphasize experiential active learning through individual projects, guest speakers, group discussions and activities, role plays, assessment, observations, and traditional instruction about the program's organizational structure and how it fits into the campus and university mission (McDaniels et al., 1994 and Mullendore & Abraham, 1993). For an expanded discussion of peer educator training see Ender and Newton (2000) and Hunter and Heath's chapter in this monograph.

What Will Students Learn?

Student leadership programs are implemented to impact other students positively. What is the result of this positive impact? For example, will students be better adjusted, more tolerant and accepting of others, learn a new concept, live healthier lifestyles, discover a career path, gain increased awareness of campus resources, plan an academic program of study, or a combination of several of these outcomes? Specificity is required here—not only so planners can describe their program to others, but also to help peer leaders understand their role. The answer to this question shapes the entire program, from selection of peer leaders to training to evaluation.

And what's in it for peer leaders? Hart (1995) notes the importance of compensation in encouraging high levels of professionalism among student leaders. Barefoot and Gardner (1993) cite popular forms of compensation at various institutions, including money, academic credit, and free residence hall accommodation; Cuseo (1993) adds that official recognition on student-activity or co-curricular transcripts is also appropriate.

More importantly, retention research indicates that students who are provided with "meaningful opportunities to contribute to [their] institution" are more likely to be satisfied with their institution (Hart, 1996, p. 37). McDaniels et al. (1994) concur: "One important way to attract and retain students is by providing opportunities for the students to become engaged in meaningful work" (p. 95). Peer leadership provides an additional learning environment that "foster[s] more growth through diverse duties and increased responsibility" (McDaniels et al., 1994, p. 95). Peer leaders' involvement at the college may also lead to increased contact with faculty members, another factor that determines student retention rates (Astin 1985; Cuseo, 1991). In addition to increasing satisfaction and persistence, peer leadership programs may en-

hance student learning opportunities. Cuseo (1991) uses past studies to note that "peer leaders can be expected to develop higher-level cognitive skills as a result of their experience" (p. 9). Students who take on leadership roles tend to become more personally involved with the campus, achieve greater understanding of how the system works, improve their grades and time management skills, and learn to manage more than one thing at a time (Roberts, 1996). In sum, peer leadership offers an invaluable learning experience by providing a "theoretical base for the practical application of their skills," while students also gain important leadership skills, learn to take responsibility, handle a wide range of professional and ethical issues, and gain a sense of self-worth (McDaniels et al., 1994, p. 98).

How Many Students Will Be Served?

How many peer leaders are needed and how will services be delivered? Programs based primarily on individual contact must determine the number of students with whom a peer leader can realistically and successfully work in a given period of time. The same is true when considering the group approach to helping. Again, determining desired learning outcomes generally suggests the most effective approach and the number of peer leaders necessary to implement this approach. In general, paraprofessionals represent a readily available and cost-effective form of providing quality student support to a greater number of students than could possibly be served by professional staff (Cuseo, 1991).

What is the Need and How Do We Document Results?

Peer leadership programs are usually implemented because institutional or program data indicate that students have a need that is unmet by existing programs. This unmet need typically leads to institutional or program outcome data that are less than satisfactory. Hart

(1996) reminds us that first-year experience studies on retention and satisfaction "indicate that the area where there is the greatest need for improvement in retaining and satisfying students is in personal services such as counseling, advising, financial aid, academic assistance, health services, and job placement" (p. 37). First, program planners must attempt to determine the need and then decide on the appropriate peer intervention(s) to close the gap between the real and the ideal. In some instances, peer leadership programs are implemented to increase the value-added dimension of attending a particular institution. That is, outcome data would indicate that the program is successful as compared to traditional benchmarks, but the institutional or program administrators desire to perform even better. After documenting need and desired outcomes, planners should determine methods for measuring those outcomes, prior to program implementation.

How Does the Program Affect Institutional Values and Mission?

Institutions of higher education are unique. Each has a mission statement espousing its values and purpose. The peer leadership program and the students who work within it are, hopefully, models of those outcomes, beliefs, and values. These students do not have to represent the final outcome(s) the college attempts to instill in its graduates; however, they should model attributes of a student in the process of becoming what the institution hopes will be outcome(s) for all students. Hart (1996) observes: "The caring environment which is created when committed upper-level students actively work to help new students sends a clear message that the university cares about student academic success and values active student involvement throughout the undergraduate experience" (p. 37). Further, Hart (1995) suggests:

It should also be noted that colleges and universities willingly use students as cleri-

cal workers, desk attendants, maintenance workers, and security guards—jobs that do not require college level training or personal judgment and initiative. Since we purport to prepare students for complex job responsibilities and leadership in society, we should be willing to employ them as peer educators and service providers, paraprofessional activities closely related to the educational purposes of our institutions. (p. 81)

Summary

Often, the theoretical underpinnings and research that provide for the success of campus programs are overlooked. By offering a historical overview of peer leadership studies, this chapter has attempted, in some small way, to bridge the gap between theory and practice. This chapter has defined the peer leadership role and has provided a theoretical base to support the practical implementation of peer leadership programs. It has demonstrated a strong history of use that suggests five critical issues for program planners to consider prior to program implementation. This discussion was intended to illuminate both the seasoned practitioner in the area of peer leadership and others who are contemplating the implementation of a peer leadership program. We trust we have met with some success.

References

Astin, A. W. (1985). *Achieving educational excellence: A critical assessment of priorities and practices in higher education.* San Francisco: Jossey-Bass.

Astin, A. W. (1993). *What matters in college? Four critical years revisited.* San Francisco: Jossey-Bass.

Barefoot, B. O. & Gardner, J. N. (1993). The freshman orientation seminar: Extending the benefits of traditional orientation. *Designing successful transitions: A guide for orienting students to college* (Monograph No. 13) (pp. 141-153). Columbia, SC: University of South Carolina,

National Resource Center for the Freshman Year Experience.

Barrow, J., & Hetherington, C. (1981). Training paraprofessionals to lead social anxiety management groups. *Journal of College Student Personnel, 22*(3), 269-273.

Berg, J. H., & Wright-Buckley, C. (1988). Effects of racial similarity and interviewer intimacy in a peer counseling analogue. *Journal of Counseling Psychology, 35,* 377-384.

Brenden, M. A. (1986). Pioneering new support systems for non-traditional baccalaureate students: Interactional advising and peer mentoring. *NACADA Journal, 6,* 77-82.

Brown, R. D. (1972). *Student development in tomorrow's higher education—A return to the academy* (Student Personnel Series No. 16). Washington, DC: American College Personnel Association.

Brown, C. R., & Myers, R. (1975). Student versus faculty curriculum advising. *Journal of College Student Personnel, 16*(3), 226-231.

Brown, W. F., & Zunker, V. G. (1966). Student counselor utilization at four-year institutions of higher learning. *Journal of College Student Personnel, 7*(1), 41-46.

Carkhuff, R. R. (1968). Differential functioning of lay and professional helpers. *Journal of Counseling Psychology, 15,* 117-126.

Carkhuff, R. R., & Truax, C. B. (1965). Lay mental health counseling: The effects of lay group counseling. *Journal of Counseling Psychology, 29,* 426-431.

Carns, A. W., Carns, M. R., & Wright, J. (1993). Students as paraprofessionals in four-year colleges and universities: Current practice compared to prior practices. *Journal of College Student Development, 34*(5), 358-363.

Chickering, A. W. (1969). *Education and identity.* San Francisco: Jossey-Bass.

Committee on the Student in Higher Education (1968). *The student in higher education.* New Haven, CT: The Hazen Foundation.

Cuseo, J. B. (1991). *The freshman orientation seminar: A research-based rationale for its value, delivery, and content* (Monograph No. 4). Columbia, SC: University of South Carolina,

National Resource Center for The Freshman Year Experience.

DeLucia, R. C. (1991). Peer-facilitated workshops: Increasing responsibilities for student paraprofessionals on campus. *Journal of College Student Development, 32,* 266-267.

Delworth, U., Sherwood, G., & Casaburri, N. (1974). *Student paraprofessionals: A working model for higher education.* Washington, DC: American College Personnel Association.

Ender, S. C. (1984). Student paraprofessionals within student affairs: The state of the art. In S. C. Ender, & R. B. Winston, Jr. (Eds.), Using students as paraprofessional staff. *New Directions for Student Services, 27* (pp. 3-21). San Francisco: Jossey-Bass.

Ender, S. C., & Newton, F. B. (2000). *Students helping students: A guide for peer educators on college campuses.* San Francisco: Jossey-Bass.

Ender, S. C., & Winston, R. B., Jr. (1984). *A national survey of student paraprofessional utilization in student affairs.* Unpublished manuscript, Kansas State University.

Frisz, R. H., & Lane, J. R. (1987). Student user evaluations of peer adviser services. *Journal of College Student Personnel, 28,* 241-245.

Hart, D. (1995). Reach-out advising strategies for first-year students. In M. L. Upcraft & G. L. Kramer (Eds.), *First-year academic advising: Patterns in the present, pathways to the future* (Monograph No. 18) (pp. 75-82). Columbia, SC: University of South Carolina, National Resource Center for the Freshman Year Experience and Students in Transition.

Hart, D. (1996). Encouraging the retention and academic success of first-year students. In W. J. Zeller, D. S. Fidler, & B. O. Barefoot (Eds.), *Residence life programs and the first-year experience* (Monograph No. 5, 2nd ed.), (pp. 35-41). Columbia, SC: University of South Carolina, National Resource Center for the Freshman Year Experience and Students in Transition.

Heath, D. H. (1968). *Growing up in college* San Francisco: Jossey-Bass.

Jones, B. E., Barnes, L. A., & Tryon-Baker, T. J. (1990). Meeting the challenges of peer education at two-year colleges. *Journal of College Student Development, 31*(5), 463-464.

Kramer, G. L., & Hardy, H. N. (1985). Facilitating the freshman experience. *College and University, 60*, 242-251.

Lewis, J. J. (1986). The black freshman network. *College and University, 61*, 135-140.

Locke, D. C., & Zimmerman, N. A. (1987). Effects of peer-counseling training on psychological maturity of black students. *Journal of College Student Personnel, 6*, 525-532.

McDaniels, R. M., Carter, J. K., Heinzen, C. J., Candrl, K. I., & Wieberg, A. M. (1994). Paraprofessionals: A dynamic staffing model. *Journal of Career Development, 21*(2), 95-109.

Mullendore, R. H., & Abraham, J. (1993). In M. L. Upcraft, R. H. Mullendore, B. O. Barefoot, & D. S. Fidler (Eds.), *Designing successful transitions: A guide for orienting students to college* (Monograph No. 13) (pp. 61-77). Columbia, SC: University of South Carolina, National Resource Center for the Freshman Year Experience.

Pascarella, E. T., & Terenzini, P. T. (1991). *How college affects students.* San Francisco: Jossey-Bass.

Powell, O. B. (1959). The student who assumes counseling responsibilities. In M. D. Hardee (Ed.), *The faculty in college counseling* (pp. 225-238). New York: McGraw-Hill.

Rabiecki, D., & Brabeck, M. M. (1985). A peer-designed peer advisement program. *Journal of College Student Personnel, 26*(1), 73-74.

Ragle, J., & Krone, K. (1989). Extending orientation: Telephone contacts by peer advisers. *Journal of College Student Personnel, 26*(1), 80-81.

Roberts, G. (1996). An African-American view of the collegiate residential experience on predominately white campuses. In W. J. Zeller, D. S. Fidler, & B. O. Barefoot (Eds.), *Residence life programs and the first-year experience* (Monograph No. 5, 2nd ed.) (pp. 55-65). Columbia, SC: University of South Carolina, National Resource Center for The Freshman Year Experience and Students in Transition.

Russell, J. H., & Skinkle, R. R. (1990). Evaluation of peer-adviser effectiveness. *Journal of College Student Development, 31*, 388-394.

Salovey, P. (1983). *A survey of campus peer counseling activities.* Paper presented at the meeting of the American College Health Association, St. Louis, MO.

Terenzini, P. T., Pascarella, E. T., & Blimling, G. S. (1996). Students' out-of-class experiences and their influence on learning and cognitive development: A literature review. *Journal of College Student Development, 37*(2), 149-162.

Winston, R. B., & Ender, S. C. (1988). Student paraprofessional utilization in college student affairs divisions. *Journal of Counseling and Student Development, 66*, 466-473.

Zunker, V. G. (1975). Students as paraprofessionals in four-year colleges and universities. *Journal of College Student Personnel, 16*(4), 282-286.

Zunker, V. G., & Brown, W. F. (1966). Comparative effectiveness of student and professional counselors. *Personnel and Guidance Journal, 44*(7), 738-743.

CHAPTER 2

LEADERSHIP EDUCATION

Vicky N. Orazem and Ashley J. Roller

Those having torches will pass them on to others.
—Plato, *The Republic*

The intent of this chapter is to establish a context for understanding leadership as a critical component of peer leader programs, to provide an overview of the historical development of leadership theory, and to give a summary of the characteristics of contemporary leadership theory that McCauley, Moxley, and Van Velsor (1998) submit are necessary for sound leadership development. Examples from five institutions ranging in size, type, and selectivity will demonstrate how McCauley et al.'s (1998) leadership model has been or can be applied to peer leader programs.

The Role of Higher Education in the Leadership Process

Why is the study of leadership important? John W. Gardner (1968), a noted scholar in this field and, during his lifetime, an exemplary leader states:

> Leaders have a significant role in creating the state of the mind that is society. They can serve as symbols of the moral unity … they can conceive and articulate goals that lift people out of their petty preoccupations, carry them above conflicts that tear a society apart and unite them in pursuit of objectives worthy of their best efforts. (p. 134)

Gardner further asserts that strong leadership is needed to advance the public interest:

> We are in desperate need of talented and highly motivated young men and women to move into the key leadership and managerial roles in government, industry, the professions and elsewhere throughout society. Our society must have the wisdom to reflect *and* the fortitude to act. It must provide the creative soil for new ideas *and* the skill and patience and hardihood to put those ideas into action. (p. 84)

As centers of learning, universities provide myriad opportunities for young people to offer service to the community, to the nation, and to humanity (Gardner, 1968). Producing quality leaders is often included as a goal in the mission statements of many universities. For example, one component of the mission statement at Harvard University (1997) states, "Education at Harvard should liberate students to explore, to create, to challenge, and to lead ...Harvard expects that the scholarship and collegiality it fosters in students will lead them in their later lives to advance knowledge, to promote understanding, and to serve society." The University of Michigan (1999) also sees leadership as vital to its mission, acknowledging the value of "developing leaders and citizens who will challenge the present and enrich the future." As a corollary, colleges and universities, as centers of learning, should serve as prime agents for creating and promoting leadership development.

Institutions across the country emphasize the importance of civic and social responsibility as a characteristic of a well-educated person. One avenue for promoting leadership skills and this sense of civic and social responsibility is through the use of upper-division students who serve as peer mentors or leaders in first-year courses and programs. According to Clark and Clark (1996), developing leaders requires a commitment to the belief that society will benefit from having capable leaders. It follows that institutions should be dedicated to producing leaders at all levels to insure a better quality of life and to effect the changes in society necessary to achieve it. Consequently, students' mentoring other students is a critical topic in leadership education and a favored strategy among leadership educators. Peer mentoring is commonly used to help upper-division students develop their leadership potential and foster professional development.

Development of Leadership Theory

During the late 1800s and early 1900s, leadership development was grounded in Darwinian principles—leaders were born with natural abilities of power and influence (Komives, Lucas, & McMahon, 1998). This movement was followed by a generation that built leadership development theories on personality traits. These theories postulated that leaders possessed particular traits of intelligence and self-confidence that distinguished them from non-leaders. In the 1950s and 1960s, popular leadership theories included both the behavioral and the situational or contingency approaches. The behavioral approach focused on managerial activities, roles, and responsibilities. Although contemporary definitions of leadership are numerous, they all involve people working together to accomplish change or to make a difference for the common good (Komives et al., 1998). The premise behind these theories purports that individuals can learn and develop leadership qualities and skills—that today's leaders are made, not born. Transformational leadership, developed by James MacGregor Burns in 1978, takes relational leadership one step further. The transformational leader is someone who motivates, challenges, and adheres to lofty ideals rather than selfish interests, with the end goal resulting in higher ethical conduct (Clark & Clark, 1996).

As a result of these changes in the conception and definition of leadership, it is now accepted that anyone, not just the genetically elite, can become a leader. Leadership is now seen as a relational process that is developed and perfected. Anyone *can* be a leader; however, not everyone *will* become a leader. Becoming a leader is an act of free will (Bennis, 1989).

Principles of Leadership Development

Foundational goals of many college and university leadership programs are to help students improve their communication and interpersonal skills, to build self-awareness and self-confidence, and to instill in these future leaders a sense of civic and social responsibility. Critical thinking, reflection, and learning intended to promote informed decision making are also integral to the development of leadership skills. According to Brookfield (1991), thinking critically is developing an awareness of the assumptions under which people think and act and the context within which actions and ideas are generated.

For McCauley et al. (1998), the first step in developing these leadership skills is self-awareness—the individual must assess his or her own individual strengths and weaknesses and work toward understanding them. Individuals must be provided with a variety of challenging experiences and must be supported and mentored throughout these endeavors. Support is a necessary ingredient for individuals to handle the struggle and pain of development, to bear the weight of the experience, and to maintain an image of oneself as someone capable of dealing with challenges (McCauley et al., 1998). The authors further assert that leadership development, like human development, is never complete, but rather a lifelong process. Implicit in this process is the belief that leaders learn as they expand their experiences. Leadership experiences are enhanced when facilitated by supportive interventions woven into their experiences. These principles of self-awareness (or self-assessment), challenge, and support are discussed in more detail below.

Self-assessment: Know Thyself

In the first *Star Wars* trilogy, Yoda takes Luke on a journey into himself, teaching him to focus and trust his own internal power. This inward journey provides Luke with self-awareness and helps him identify his abilities, strengths, and weaknesses. In the process of the journey, Luke develops a sense of trust in his abilities and in his level of effectiveness (Komives, et al., 1998). Leadership education begins with a similar process of self-discovery.

According to Bennis (1989), "know[ing] thyself...means separating who you are and who you want to be, from what the world thinks you are and wants you to be" (p. 54). Self-knowledge and self-intervention are lifelong processes. Bennis (1989) postulates four critical features of self-knowledge: (a) You are

your own best teacher; (b) you must accept responsibility and blame no one; (c) you can learn anything you want to learn; and (d) true understanding comes from reflecting on your experience. Self-assessment, or self-knowledge, is important because it gives individuals an understanding of their current skills, strengths, weaknesses, and leadership effectiveness. This involves examining their individual qualities and asking such questions as:

« Do I feel a sense of responsibility to others?
« Do I have a purpose in life?
« What am I doing well? Where do I need to improve?
« What are others' views of me? Do peers look to me as a leader?
« How do my behaviors impact others?
« How am I doing relative to my goals?
« What's important to me?
« Am I qualified? Do I have the stamina to accept the challenge?

Bennis (1989) attests that leaders are self-directed and claims, "You make your life your own by understanding it" (p. 71). He postulates the following formula for leadership: self-awareness = self-knowledge = self-possession = self-control = self-expression.

Challenge: Learning through Experience

Learning about leadership and having experiences in leading and following are critical to the development of leadership skills and style (Clark & Clark, 1996). According to McCauley et al. (1998), challenging developmental experiences force people to work outside of their comfort zones. People feel challenged when they encounter situations that demand skills and abilities beyond their current capabilities or when the situation is confusing, ambiguous,

> Leadership experiences are enhanced when facilitated by supportive interventions woven into their experiences.

or characterized by conflict. The premise here lies in the fact that leadership abilities develop when one fully participates in a challenging learning environment. Learning to lead is learning by doing (McCauley et al., 1998). When placed in a challenging environment, students develop their leadership skills by improving their ability to interact socially, by modeling effective communication, by fostering effective group dynamics, and by improving their problem-solving skills.

Support

According to McCauley et al. (1998), supporting the emerging leader is an essential component of leadership training. While experiences can stretch individuals and highlight their strengths and weaknesses, these experiences are most powerful when augmented with a strong element of support. Challenging experiences motivate individuals to learn and grow—the element of support sends the message that the emerging leader's efforts are valued. Without support, the experience may overwhelm the leader, as opposed to offering a new opportunity for learning and growth. The model offered by McCauley et al. (1998) suggests that the leadership process is enhanced when facilitated by interventions in the learning, growth, and change processes of individuals. This leadership model suggests that practitioners can enhance the learning process by providing a strong element of support. If individuals are to learn from their experiences, they must receive ongoing feedback while struggling with the challenge of learning (McCauley et al., 1998).

> ...leadership abilities develop when one fully participates in a challenging learning environment.

Leaders, Mentors, and Peers: The Connection

Exemplary leadership education programs are ones that provide mentoring roles to novice leaders as they practice the skills of self-assessment, challenge, and support. Mentoring, in turn, prepares aspiring leaders to perpetuate and sustain the tradition of leading into the next generation. Helpers—educators, counselors, colleagues, and friends—assist individuals in becoming critical thinkers in a variety of settings by challenging them to interpret and question ideas and actions from new points of view (Brookfield, 1991).

Mitchell (1998), Vice-Chancellor at the University of California-Los Angeles, sees mentoring as an integral component in leadership development: "The people I know who are great leaders are great mentors. I don't think it is an accident; in fact, I am fairly sure that one cannot be a truly great leader without being a great mentor..." (p. 48). He regards mentoring as a form of teaching, an essential element of leadership. Mentoring, he says, "is the ability to transfer skills and knowledge...to lead others to reach beyond previously assumed limits of understanding, perspective and will" (p. 48). Moreover, mentoring involves growth: "Leaders who do not grow, soon cease to be leaders, and novices who do not grow cannot become leaders" (p. 48). Mitchell suggests, "Good mentorship is good leadership, and leadership without mentorship is shallow and sterile. All of us who have enjoyed mentorship in its pure form must commit to continuing the tradition and passing the gift along" (p. 48).

Best Practices

The programs described in this section underscore the excellent work colleges and universities do to provide leadership opportunities for upper-division students, while fostering the development of intellectual and personal goals for all students. These exemplary programs also focus on developing the leadership skills and traits in upper-division students discussed earlier in this chapter: communication and interpersonal skills, self-awareness and confidence, a sense of civic and social responsibility, and critical thinking and reflective abilities. The majority of examples provided here focus on leadership development through peer instruction in first-year seminar programs.

Each program highlighted in this section may be defined in relation to McCauley et al.'s (1999) model of leadership and is described here in terms of self-assessment, challenge, and support. The challenging experience is framed as the specific activity or assignment for the student leader. The next section describes how the student leader assesses his or her ability to perform or carry out the challenge. Each example concludes with a description of the support provided by faculty, staff, and administration to assist the peers in their developmental experience. Contact information is provided for each program.

Montana State University-Bozeman General Studies Peer Leader Program

The General Studies Freshman Seminar (GENS 101V) at Montana State University-Bozeman serves approximately 600 undeclared first-year students. Upperclass peer leaders are an integral component of this course. While these peer instructors lend student perspective to the planning, delivery, and impact of GENS 101V, they also gain leading and mentoring experiences. They are responsible for developing a health and wellness component for the course and for assisting students in the preparation of a 25–minute group presentation on an issue of social equity. Peer instructors work closely with faculty to enhance the academic, cultural, and social experiences for the first-year students in the GENS 101V course.

The Challenge

« As a leading experience, peers are required to create, develop, and implement two to three days of course curriculum on health and wellness activities for GENS 101V.

« The goal of a group project is to help students interpret events, situations, and conflicts from diverse cultural perspectives during which they examine their own beliefs, attitudes, and ideas on multicultural issues. The peer instructors assist the students as they plan, research, and implement their group project, while remaining outside the team. Throughout this mentoring experience, peers are expected to mediate conflict, provide objective feedback, model effective communication, and foster effective group dynamics.

Self-assessment

« The peer instructors assess their strengths and weaknesses in curriculum writing and development and in communication and presentation skills. They are asked to assess any areas that might be "hot buttons" for them.

« They must assess their oral and written communication skills, library research skills, and group facilitation skills.

Support

« Guest speakers from across the university community present information on aspects of wellness (i.e., alcohol and other drug programming; sexually transmitted diseases; rape prevention; and diet, nutrition, and exercise needs). The peer instructors schedule these guest speakers and provide students with a handbook of suggested activities.

« The instructional team meets to discuss individual expectations for the project. They then meet with each group to set and define expectations and to brainstorm topics. Library personnel provide guidance for topic research.

Contact Information:

Vicki Orazem
Freshman Seminar Coordinator
General Studies Department

418 Reid Hall, MSU
Bozeman, MT 59717
Phone: (406) 994-6435
E-mail: vorazem@montana.edu

Champlain College
Peer Mentoring for Freshman Focus

Peer Mentoring for Freshman Focus, Champlain College's first-year seminar, began in 1995. Approximately 250 students enroll in 12 sections of the program each fall semester. From this pool of students, the seminar faculty recommend individuals whom they believe show the most promise as leaders, to take a follow-up, one-credit class. This class is taught during the spring semester and is entitled Leadership in Action (LIA).

LIA is designed to train students for peer mentorship positions as well as to help them acquire an appreciation for the complexities of leadership. Over the years, the class has evolved into one that is rich with readings, discussions, and many interactive exercises geared toward exploring general issues of leadership. Topics such as the nature of leadership, ethics and values, power, leadership styles, followership readiness levels, and college-student developmental theory are presented and examined.

The Challenge

« Since peer instructors work with their Freshman Focus section for the entire semester to plan each session and lead the class during designated activities, they usually develop strong out-of-class relationships with their students. Consequently, these peers often grapple with issues of authority and responsibility. This is further complicated by the fact that peer instructors are usually only one year older than the first-year students. The question of "balance" is often discussed. Which behaviors are appropriate outside the classroom and which are not are perennial issues.

« Peer instructors must learn how to motivate a group, how to organize an activity from start to finish, and how to manage a variety of student personalities. Each peer instructor must negotiate a working relationship with his or her Freshman Focus teaching partner and manage differences in ways beneficial to both.

Self-assessment

« In the LIA course, peer instructors receive a weekly grade for reaction papers on readings that address various leadership topics. They also complete a leadership profile, which helps them identify their strengths and weaknesses. Classmates and the instructor rate the peers on the presentation of a 15–minute activity. Additionally, the instructor meets with these students to discuss their ongoing progress in the class and to determine if they are well-suited for the role of peer instructor.

« Peer instructors are also evaluated on a reflection paper and earn one credit for completing the final portion of the leadership experience.

Support

« Peer instructors are given the opportunity to meet with former peer mentors and be introduced to their responsibilities and to specific skills necessary for becoming effective peer mentors. These include listening skills, verbal and nonverbal communication, and assertiveness.

« The LIA class provides the initial support for the peer mentors through relevant reading materials and by providing ample opportunity to practice communication skills and classroom activities. Ongoing support is provided through the Peer-Mentoring Seminar where mentors share triumphs and concerns with their fellow mentors and the instructor of the seminar.

Contact Information:

Shelli Goldsweig
Director of Freshman Focus
Champlain College
PO Box 670
Burlington, VT 05402
Phone: (802) 865-6427
E-mail: goldswei@champlain.edu

Worcester Polytechnic Institute
Peer Learning Assistants in Cooperative Learning Courses

The Peer Learning Assistant (PLA) model was developed to improve both educational quality and faculty productivity in large courses being taught in a lecture mode. With support from the Davis Educational Foundation, small grants were offered to faculty to restructure their courses in a cooperative learning (CL) format. To ensure this change does not pose an increase of faculty workload, PLAs are employed to facilitate group process and group dynamics in large introductory courses where CL is used.

Models of PLA use vary from course to course. A PLA is typically assigned to work with three to five student groups, for one or two class periods per week and for out-of-class group meetings. PLAs have no responsibility for grading. In this model, faculty are managers of the learning process in which students take a more active role, and PLAs provide the day-to-day facilitation necessary to make the process work on a large scale.

Results of this experiment have shown that students in PLA-assisted courses learn more and get better grades both in PLA-assisted courses and in courses later in their academic careers. Further, evidence suggests that these students are more likely to persist at WPI and to graduate in four years than students who did not take PLA-assisted courses.

The Challenge

PLAs take on roles that capitalize on the fact that peers are both more available and generally more approachable than faculty. However, PLAs are not group leaders: The responsibility for completing group projects rests squarely with the students. PLAs are not tutors, although they will answer questions about course content if asked. PLAs facilitate group process and group dynamics without crossing the line into group leadership. Their biggest challenge is to decide when and how to intervene and when to let the group struggle a little. Their role involves the use of people skills more than disciplinary knowledge. PLAs help students find resources and develop the group organization to tackle open-ended projects. They also help to identify and facilitate early resolution of interaction problems in their groups.

Self-assessment

Students at the end of each course evaluate their PLAs, and PLAs conduct ongoing self-assessment. They often report what they tried and what worked at course staff meetings. When asked to rate the value of their PLA experience, almost all noted positive impacts on their leadership, teamwork, and oral and written communication skills.

Support

PLAs are trained for 10 hours prior to the beginning of the course in which they work. Training varies from course to course, but contains a large component of self-awareness, motivation theory, cooperative learning, helping skills, and role playing activities. All of these elements assist with the interpersonal aspects of the job. Experienced PLAs are always part of the course team, and they serve as informal mentors to new PLAs. Course staff members meet with the group one hour per week to discuss group and course logistical issues. There are also frequent e-mail and face-to-face contacts between the PLAs and course instructors.

Contact information:

Judith E. Miller
Professor of Biology & Biotechnology and Director of Educational Development
Worcester Polytechnic Institute
100 Institute Rd.
Worcester, MA 01609
Phone: (508) 831-5579
E-mail: jmiller@wpi.edu
Project report at http://www.WPI.EDU/Academics/CED/reports.html#davis

University of Colorado at Colorado Springs Junior Teaching Assistants

Junior Teaching Assistants at the University of Colorado at Colorado Springs take a three-hour upper division course on teaching and learning while they are mentoring the 15 first-year students in their section of the first-year seminar course. The Freshman Seminar Program pays the students' tuition for the course. JTAs apply for these positions and are chosen from a competitive pool of applicants each year.

Challenge

For JTAs, the biggest challenge is that they must maintain close contact with their first-year students throughout the semester while juggling class assignments in their concurrent teaching/learning course.

Self-assessment

JTA's negotiate a detailed contract with their faculty sponsors, meet formally with each first-year student twice during the semester, e-mail summaries of these meetings to the director, and e-mail their first-year students frequently. They are required to do journal research, write a philosophy of education statement, and submit a final paper summarizing their JTA experience.

Support

This team model (four faculty and JTAs to a topic group) encourages JTAs to support one another. JTAs meet with the director in topic group teams (a team-teaching model is used). They are also supported by the director and by their faculty sponsors. The response from JTAs to this leadership development experience has been overwhelmingly positive.

Contact Information:

Constance Staley
Director, Freshman Seminar Program
Professor of Communication
Columbine Hall 3057
University of Colorado
Colorado Springs, CO 80933
Phone: (719) 262-4123
E-mail: cstaley@brain.uccs.edu

University of Sunshine Coast (Formerly Sunshine Coast University College) Mentoring Program

Sunshine Coast University College (SCUC) was established in Fall 1996. It was anticipated that new students might easily feel lost in an unfamiliar and rapidly changing and developing system. Hence, a student mentoring program was introduced as a high priority for the first orientation period of the university. Soon after, an orientation mentoring scheme using past, successful second-year students entitled SCUC GURUs was established. It offered students a network to access information about university life and to develop valuable, supportive relationships.

GURUs worked with small groups of new

students for a few hours each day during orientation, assisting them with their transition into university life. These sessions included help with enrollment procedures, short tours of university facilities and mini-workshops on topics such as studying at SCUC, goal setting, time management, and notetaking.

The Challenge

The feedback obtained from the first orientation program indicated that more than 30% of new students were the first in their immediate families to enroll in a university. This was and continues to be a challenge for the GURUs as they seek to provide services for new students and fulfill the program mission to:

« support social and academic integration
« develop a sense of belonging to a community
« facilitate active participation in the life of the university

Another major aim has been to enable new students to meet others with whom they can form a supportive relationship both within their cohort and with other, more experienced students (second-year students). Where possible, students are grouped according to their intended area of study and with a GURU from the same area (e.g., business, arts, and applied sciences).

Self-assessment

« Participation in this program revealed that the benefits for the SCUC GURU program included: (a) development of leadership skills, (b) improved facilitation, (c) improved study skills, (d) improved group management skills, (e) improved self-confidence and self-esteem, and (f) improved understanding of learning and teaching processes and curriculum.
« The program enhanced contact between academic staff and the GURUs and increased the awareness of the personal input and impact that they can have within the SCUC community.

Support

The Core Units Coordinator and the Learning Assistance Advisor supported the SCUC GURUs academically, socially, and administratively. They acted in a mentoring role for these student leaders by encouraging and interacting with them personally and by attempting to enhance their personal experience and development through participation in the program and through their activities within the SCUC community.

The Core Units, Student Services, and Learning Assistance Offices made resources and materials available to the GURUs and their student groups through the Core Units Coordinator and the Learning Assistance Advisor.

Training for the role of GURU was conducted during the week prior to Orientation Week and included the following topics:

« Exploration of the SCUC GURU's role as mentor
« Communication and group facilitation skills
« Adult learning principles
« Cultural differences in learning
« Students with disabilities
« Approaches to study
« Self-assessment

Resources and coaching were provided for student leaders to help them present mini-workshops on studying at SCUC, time management, goal setting, and notetaking.

Contact Information:

Carol Bowie
Griffith University
Nathan Queensland, 4111
Australia
E-mail: C.Bowie@mailbox.gu.edu.au

Conclusion

Colleges and universities, as centers of learning, are natural training grounds for leadership development, and many colleges and universities provide leadership training and courses for leadership development for their students. The developmental approaches offered by the institutions highlighted above are powerful and replicable models of education allowing for clear-eyed self-assessment, appropriate challenge, and valuable support. These models offer lessons for those involved in leadership education and all educators.

References

Bennis, W. (1989). *On becoming a leader.* New York: Addison-Wesley.

Brookfield, S. D. (1991). *Developing critical thinkers.* San Francisco: Jossey-Bass.

Clark, K. E., & Clark, M. B. (1996). *Choosing to lead* (2nd ed.). Greensboro, NC: Center for Creative Leadership.

Gardner, J. W. (1968). *No easy victories.* New York: Harper & Row.

Harvard University. (1997). *Mission of Harvard College.* Cambridge, MA: Author. Retrieved September 13, 2000 from the World Wide Web: http://www.harvard.edu/help/noframes/faq110_nf.html

Komives, S., Lucas, N., & McMahon, T. R. (1998). *Exploring leadership: For college students who want to make a difference.* San Francisco: Jossey-Bass.

McCauley, C. D., Moxley, R. S., & Velsor, E. V. (Eds.). (1998). *Center for creative leadership development.* San Francisco: Jossey-Bass.

Mitchell, T. (1998). Mentorship as leadership. *Change, 30*(1), 48.

University of Michigan. (1999). *Mission statement.* Retrieved September 13, 2000 from the World Wide Web: http://www.umich.edu/UM-Mission.html

CHAPTER 3

THE SUCCESSFUL OPERATION OF A PEER LEADERSHIP PROGRAM

Christopher Lynch*

The experience of the new student in college is like going to visit a culture with its own language, values, and expectations for interaction. Gaining a foothold in a sometimes strange land can be difficult for students, but administrators have valuable resources in peer leader programs to help students navigate this territory. The peer leaders model cultural codes while acting as translators of the new language so that new students do not become marginalized and frustrated.

The role of translator, however, is not an easy one because the peer leaders often get caught in the middle between the students and the institution. Persons-in-the-middle need to understand and respect all perspectives, but at the same time these persons might not be complete insiders to any perspective. Persons-in-the-middle are caught in a tension between pleasing or hurting one side or the other and usually do not have much power because they are treated with a certain amount of suspicion by both sides. When this happens the temptation is to choose one limited perspective or give up the job by mid-semester.

This chapter offers suggestions for reducing unrealistic expectations of peer leaders which may reinforce their limited perspectives. These suggestions include role clarification, training, contracting, team meetings, and opportunities for self-reflection. The chapter also highlights some issues that threaten the maintenance of peer leadership programs and concludes with a discussion of attitudes that administrators need to develop in order to maintain a positive program for peer leaders. These suggestions are based, in part, on my experiences as director of the first-year seminar program at Kean University. The program is run out of the Center for New Students, which also facilitates orientation programs, an information center, and an advisement center for registration. The office employs approximately 65 peer leaders who work in the office and assist with the first-year seminar program. These suggestions are supported by ideas from extensive interviews with fellow administrators of student leader programs from around the country.

*The author thanks peer leader coordinators at the universities described and Peggy Melchione, Patricia Clark, and Lauren Mastrobuono, from the Center for New Students at Kean University, for their input in this article.

Role Clarification and Expectations

From the initial job interview student leaders should have a clear sense of their role as it relates to the program goal. Having current student leaders present at the interview, modeling leadership skills by the depth of their questions or by stressing the importance of being on time and dressing appropriately, is one way to give a sense of role right from the beginning. From the outset, supervisors need to stress those behaviors (e.g., alcohol and other drug use) which are incompatible with the role of peer leader.

Clarifying Program Goals

Training provides another opportunity for program coordinators to outline expectations, often in more detail than the interview setting allows. Clearly defined goals for the program presented at training and evaluated at team meetings provide peer leaders with a sense of purpose and stability. The alternative, not highlighting goals, results in a program where peer leaders are likely to become confused and where new students receive inconsistent messages. These goals are made more concrete by identifying specific performance objectives, which might include: helping to plan the class, making weekly announcements, keeping records of student class attendance, developing mini-lectures or leading class discussions, meeting with students on an individual basis, collecting tickets as evidence of attendance at special events, serving as a receptionist at the office or information desk, etc. Program administrators must prioritize goals and performance objectives according to the program needs, helping leaders to know which responsibilities are most important. A student leader handbook is a good place to list these priorities so that leaders have a constant reminder of expectations. Program administrators should not assume, however, that leaders will read it on their own. A review of the handbook, highlighting the significance of each goal, should be built into training sessions.

A peer leader might be tempted to identify with the students' immediate needs rather than the long-range goals, such as when the "helpful" peer leader encourages students to take the "easier" or more "fun" professors or courses rather than those that might be more central to a student's academic or career path (Habley, 1984). If students have decided to become peer leaders because their experience as a student in a first-year course was "fun," they may struggle when partnered with an instructor or program whose goals may stress "challenge" as the way to academic excellence. Administrators need to instill in leaders the sense that these goals are worth pursuing. Sharing success stories and giving a rationale behind goals are ways program coordinators can do this (Larson & LaFasto, 1989).

Not only should the goals set standards, but they should also be realistic. The program goals should be evaluated at periodic points over the semester. Clarifying and prioritizing which goals are most important will strengthen a program; however, program administrators should be careful not to overwhelm the peer leaders with too many priorities. When possible, peer leaders should have the opportunity to participate in program goal setting. As Kouzes and Posner (1999) suggest, practice in goal setting is fundamental for training in the professional world and prepares the new student leaders for their future.

Defining the Job

A clearly written job description should help clarify situations where the goals and performance expectations appear to be in conflict. The job description should emphasize that the peer leader represents the entire institution to the new students. I know of one case where a peer leader told the class that a letter from the university president was unimportant. In other instances, peer leaders may warn new students away from health services, certain organizations, or academic programs. The peer leader should be an unbiased source of information, a promoter of all aspects of the campus community. This institutional role also puts the peer leaders in a position where maintaining confidentiality and remaining open to students gives their job credibility (Habley, 1984). At the same time, a job description helps the institution keep in perspective any unreal expectations it may have about what peer leaders can be expected to do. Tensions may arise between peer leaders and program coordinators when the peer leaders, who are often campus leaders, become committed to many extracurricular activities that pull them away from their work responsibilities. These tensions may escalate at the end of the semester when the student leaders are preparing for their own exams and writing papers, especially because the peer leaders have less time to help new students who are experiencing similar end-of-the-semester stressors. Southwest Missouri State University, using peer leaders in its first-year seminar program since 1996, helps minimize these tensions by not allowing first-year seminar student leaders to serve as resident advisors during their first year as peer leaders.

Training

Training is essential to role clarification because it is a time to provide rationale, communicate expectations, and develop performance objectives. Further, participation in training suggests the level of commitment a peer leader will have for a program as a whole. One challenge is getting busy peer leaders to attend the whole training program. Some programs pay peer leaders to attend ($6.25 to $7.50 per hour), but extensive training could strain a program's budget. A second way to encourage attendance is by giving academic credit for participation. Kent State University lays the foundation for its program by choosing over 150 peer leaders after a screening course that offers trainees two credits toward graduation on a pass or fail basis. As a part of the course, all prospective peer leaders at Kent State design at least nine lesson plans and

teach a 10- to 15-minute micro-class. Team leaders conclude the course by overseeing a two-hour final exam created by the program supervisor. The team leaders in consultation with the program supervisor grade students who attend all sessions of the class. The course is taught and supervised by co-ed pairs of experienced peer leaders. The experienced peer leaders receive three upper division credit hours and a letter grade from the peer leader supervisor after participating in their own training sessions. New peer leaders will meet weekly with experienced peer leaders during the semester that they teach a first-year seminar, and they receive another two credits for teaching the course. The screening course eliminates trainees who are unlikely to take their responsibilities seriously and ensures that the peer leaders who are selected are willing to commit time and energy to the program.

> Administrators need to instill in leaders the sense that these goals are worth pursuing. Sharing success stories and giving rationales behind goals are ways program coordinators can do this (Larson & LaFasto, 1989).

When peer leaders play significant roles in training, they serve as models for the new leaders and reinforce the goals of the program. At the same time, acting as training facilitators reduces the resistance of peer leaders who are reluctant to come to training after their first year because it gives them a new role and reinforces their commitment to the program.

Contracting

Laying a solid foundation through role clarification and training is central to the success of a peer leader program. The student leader often approaches the experience in an idealistic way that can raise unreal expectations about academia. New peer leaders are often excited about their new leadership roles and are easily shocked when they encounter the teaching partner who does not show up for class or fails to mirror their enthusiasm for the class. Others might encounter the autocratic professor who treats them as a teacher's aid or merely as a "gopher," rather than as someone with a key classroom role. These students easily become cynical when confronted with a reality that differs so sharply from their expectations.

A way to reduce potential conflicts and unrealistic expectations is to have the peer leader and instructor sit down before the semester begins and work out a mutually agreed upon contract, describing their roles in class and the relationship they hope to build with each other. The contract helps the teaching team clarify roles and reduces unreal expectations they have of each other (Kurvink, 1993). Further, the development and negotiation process provides an opportunity for the peer leader to get to know the instructor as a person and vice versa.

Instructors may devote all their energy to the new students, but they need to remember they also have a mentoring role with the peer leader who is learning to be a leader. At the same time, the peer leader has much to teach the instructor. Because the peer leader often sees the class in a way closer to that of new students, the students are more likely to approach the peer leader with questions and concerns. Often they will listen to a peer leader rather than an instructor. Further, the peer leader can monitor how the instructor's presence influences the class and how the students are assimilating into the academic environment. Instructors should request frequent feedback from peer leaders on the class climate. Instructors gain valuable insights, often resulting in positive changes in pedagogical strategies not only in the first-year seminar but in their other classes as well. Knowledge of these peer leader roles empowers the team as a whole.

On the other hand, the role of the student peer leader in a professional department can become intimidating to the professional staff (Blackburn-Smith & Lembo, 1998). In their enthusiasm to succeed, the peer leaders might want to change the system before they fully understand the institutional bureaucracy. They are still learning to share feedback with an instructor, and the experienced professional might tire of input that seems to come too frequently and often without diplomacy. Instructors can become threatened by the peer leaders' level of competence and impose a stifling authoritarianism to keep them in their place as students. Moreover, if an instructor does not model respect for the peer leader, the peer leader is less likely to receive respect from students. At Kean University, contracts include a commitment on the part of the instructor to support the student leader by encouraging new students to be on time if they have appointments with the peer leader outside of class time. Beyond this, contracts should incorporate the following information:

« Each contract should include specific information about when, where, and how long the instructor and peer leader will meet each week. Creating a contract provides an opportunity to work out a plan for the next class with each individual's responsibility clearly defined. At the same time it puts a mechanism in place where both parties critique and share feedback from the previous class.

« The contract should also contain information on what actions each person will be responsible for in the class. Included here are issues of how each person wants to be addressed during class. Where will they sit? If one is absent, how will he or she notify the other?

« The contract should include individual responsibilities. For example, the instructor might be solely responsible for grading, while the peer leader will be responsible for keeping an attendance record, planning and delivering classes on selected topics, and arranging out-of-class activities.

Before creating the contract, two steps should be taken. First, new peer leaders and instructors need to be oriented to the potential perspective and needs of the other. Since this relationship involves mutual teamwork, it is helpful for experienced peer leaders and instructors to share their past experiences, expectations, and concerns at a training session for new peer leaders and instructors. Once these issues have been addressed, the purpose and key elements of a contract can be outlined. Because the student population at Kean University represents 180 nationalities, Kean uses the contract as a way to help bridge the differing cultural perspectives in its 65 instructional teams. Kean's Freshman Seminar instructor-peer manual contains sample contracts, and sometimes the peer-instructor team will decide to sign one of these contracts after discussion of the issues. The instructor team has the option to create its own contract after studying the sample contracts. (See Appendix D for sample contracts.) They may also develop it in response to specific questions regarding their relationship and how they will handle any conflicts. The program administrator provides peer leaders and instructors with questionnaires. (See sample questionnaires in Appendix C.)

A second concern to be addressed before developing the contract is building rapport between members of the instructional team. This creates a climate conducive to listening and mutual respect. When instructors and peer leaders meet informally over lunch during the summer, rapport building begins. At the Kean University training, a questionnaire exploring personal interests, hobbies, and likes and dislikes is distributed to and completed by both parties. The information on these sheets is then shared with the other partner before writing the contract. These icebreakers build a climate that encourages genuine dialogue, making contract negotiations easier.

Once the contract is developed, a signed copy is kept on file in the supervisor's office, and a copy is given to each member of the team as a reminder of his or her accountability to the other. Kean University recommends that instructor teams review the contract after the first month of classes to assess its effectiveness and to make any necessary changes.

Negotiating Group Dynamics

A study of communication in organizations shows that the most common complaint from fellow workers regards associates who are more self-oriented than team-oriented (Larson & LaFasto, 1992). The formation of cliques on the peer leader team is a good example of this behavior. Ensuring that peer leaders work with all the other peer leaders through icebreakers or discussions at training should discourage the formation of cliques. A student leader must learn that the best leaders are flexible enough to allow others to lead and that every job is important for the sake of the team (Blackburn-Smith & Lembo, 1998). Program coordinators can model this by demonstrating a willingness to do some of the dirty work themselves, sending the message that everyone is working together for the common good (Blackburn-Smith & Lembo, 1998). A willingness to do unpleasant or monotonous tasks teaches peer leaders that leaders do not always have to be in the spotlight and that all jobs are important. Working with peer leaders on routine tasks, like stuffing envelopes, helps build rapport, which might make a peer leader more comfortable approaching the staff coordinator with a problem. Lauren Pernetti from Kent State notes, "If the students like you, they will work for you."

All peer leaders bring skills to the program with which they are involved. Good supervisors recognize such skills and allow students to develop in these areas. Early interviews might elicit from the potential peer leader areas where he or she might have a specialization that enhances the program, giving him or her a sense of providing a needed contribution. While any program will want to encourage individual success, such success needs to be balanced with a willingness to do the routine tasks like stuffing envelopes for an orientation program or duplicating materials that take the peer leader out of the limelight.

> Neither instructors nor peer leaders can be always "on" in the classroom. But for a generation reared in the television age, this is not an easy idea to accept and becomes a deep fear many new peer leaders have about themselves. They do not want to be boring.

Moreover, peer leaders should be reminded that each person, from the campus officers to the newest peer leaders, must work together and share their need for each other. Peer leaders can easily get in over their heads as they encounter the co-dependent student or the student in personal crisis. Peer leaders need to learn to reach out, seek referrals, and ask for help from professional staff members and other peer leaders.

Team Meetings

Team meetings encourage dialogue and help the staff gain a sense of the overall operation of the program within each class. Meetings also become important in large programs where supervisors cannot meet with peer leaders on an individual basis. At Kean, the meetings last about an hour and are held monthly; attendance at these meetings is expected. The meetings serve a number of functions: (a) to alert peer leaders to upcoming campus events of which they should make their students aware, (b) to call peer leaders to accountability if expectations are not being met, and (c) to provide peer leaders with an opportunity to share successes or concerns with other team members. Team meetings also help a supervi-

sor uncover and address hidden agendas that may negatively impact the program. While providing peer leaders with an opportunity to share, supervisors should oversee the creation of an agenda to avoid having the meeting turn into a gossip session. Moreover, because the discussion of course issues may involve individual students, peer leaders must agree to keep any issue discussed at meetings confidential. Student leaders with problems that require more time to resolve and are different from team issues should meet with the supervisor at another time.

Team meetings are vital for empowering the peer leaders. Even though instructor and peer leader build a relationship and share mutual responsibilities, the instructors have more power by virtue of their position, experience, and knowledge of the institution and because they are most often solely responsible for grading students. Team meetings allow time for peer leaders to raise frustrations in dealing with an instructor before they escalate. If a problem arises between peer leader and instructor, the support staff and other peer leaders act as coaches to help resolve the problem.

The meetings can also provide a forum for discussing classroom performance. Georgia Institute of Technology, using 150 peer leaders per year, has a number of peer leaders working together as a team in a class of 35 students. The professor supervises the peer leaders, and each student leader is responsible for specific first-year students in the class. The peer leaders also design and deliver team presentations to the group as a whole. California State University at Long Beach also places a number of peer leaders in a single classroom. Three peer mentor coordinators and experienced peer leaders visit each class on a regular basis to critique the quality of peer leadership. Because classroom observations can cause anxiety, peer leaders need to understand the importance of observations in maintaining quality instruction and should receive both positive and negative feedback. The information is shared with the classroom team and then common issues are discussed at the larger team meetings. Because this program employs at least two student leaders in each classroom, ways to avoid becoming a "stage hog" in the classroom also need to be addressed.

Strengthening the Instructor-Peer Leader Team

Ideally, the spirit of the larger team will spill over into the classroom so that the peer leader and instructor become an effective team. Peer leaders should be reminded that sometimes even full-time professionals lose confidence and need support from their teaching partners. One peer leader whispered to a new instructor in the middle of her class exercise, "They're bored! Do something else!" This sent the instructor into a panic, as she did not want to bore the students. Instructors need helpful ideas rather than judgmental criticism rooted in the unreal expectation that they can never err. Neither instructors nor peer leaders can be always "on" in the classroom. But for a generation reared in the television age, this is not an easy idea to accept and becomes a deep fear many new peer leaders have about themselves. They do not want to be boring. They need to realize that the success or the failure of the class does not rest solely on their shoulders. The teacher or peer leader as entertainer might not be as effective as the instructor or peer leader who is genuinely interested in the new students.

Mediating Conflicts

Sometimes, a peer leader has problems with students. The peer leader is encouraged to inform the instructor so that they can work together to resolve the issue. Sometimes a co-peer leader is sent in as moral support for a student leader in a stressful situation. At other times, the peer leader is advised to talk to individual students or the class about the conflict. If expectations have become cloudy, roles between the new student and peer leader are then clarified.

Conflicts may also arise between the instructor and the peer leader. As a first option, it is usually best to let the student and instructor resolve their differences because the entrance of a third party can escalate a conflict and create a hostile environment. If the peer leader has difficulty resolving the conflict on his or her own, a member of the support staff may serve as a mediator. The mediator's job is to keep the conversation going between the two parties, but he or she should remain neutral in seeking a resolution. As a final option in extreme cases where dialogue has broken down, the support staff becomes arbitrator defining how the situation should be resolved (Donohue & Kolt, 1992).

Using Senior Peer Leaders as Team Leaders

Choosing experienced peer leaders as team leaders becomes a way to reward these students for a job well done, while helping to organize the program more efficiently. Team leaders coordinate a small group of student leaders and serve as a liaison with the administrator. The administrator who is unable to be present at every team meeting communicates information and receives feedback through team leader meetings. At the same time, team leaders have new experiences that will help them in their personal and professional lives.

Self-Reflection

Research shows that people learn best through experience because they move beyond passive learning and begin to internalize values (MacGregor, 1993). In addition, the changing workplace requires not so much a specific skill set as it does a person who can reflect on alternatives and adapt to changing circumstances (Schön, 1983). One way to call peer leaders to accountability and to help them become self-directed learners is to ask them to evaluate themselves and the quality of their work. Keeping a weekly log and conducting an exit interview at the end of the semester provide opportunities for the peer leader to reflect. At the same time, self-reflection activities help the staff monitor performance.

The peer leader writes a log entry after each class and addresses a few basic questions: What did I contribute to class this week? What problems did I encounter? What could be done differently? A staff member is assigned to read the entries each week. This is also a way to uncover problem areas that the peer leader might be uncomfortable voicing in meetings with the team or supervisor.

An exit interview conducted with each peer leader at the end of the semester also encourages self-reflection. The peer leader responds in writing to a series of questions and then discusses the content with the support staff who use this information to evaluate his or her performance over the course of the semester. A peer leader is invited to return the next semester based on this interview. (Sample exit interview questions are included in Appendix E.)

Creating a Learning Climate through Attitudes for Success

A peer leadership program is a work in progress because with so many personalities involved, new issues are constantly arising. For this reason, the program administrator needs to have the flexibility to adapt to changing situations and to enforce a positive learning environment. In light of this, one should seek to instill certain key attitudes in peer leaders, faculty instructors, and administrative support staff.

The first attitude to nurture is a willingness to laugh at oneself, which involves a confidence that gives permission to make mistakes, to apologize, to be humbled, and to experience failure without letting it overwhelm one in a dysfunctional way. An ability to laugh at oneself, as an administrator or instructor, also means allowing students to become teachers and recognizing that learning is an ongoing process. Learning to laugh at oneself gives students the confidence to explore and discover new worlds. Peer leadership programs have the unique possibility of teaching this message because students can see education from both sides. Few other academic programs have such a rich teaching tool. In fact, the academic world frequently teaches students to avoid mistakes and failure by placing a stigma on low grades or emphasizing the product over the process of learning. Giving students the freedom to make mistakes opens the door to creativity and initiative, qualities that employers value (Blackburn-Smith & Lembo, 1998).

One of the keys to a successful organization is the ability to affirm employees' worth. If employees feel valued, they will be committed to their jobs and work to achieve their highest potential (Kouzes & Posner, 1999). Peer leaders should be reminded that they are doing valuable work in the midst of unique tensions.

Affirmation also involves knowing students by name and taking time to show interest in their personal lives. Knowing names is not always easy, especially in large programs, but placing a bulletin board at the entrance of the office with a picture and the name of each peer leader can facilitate this process. Not only will this make the students feel important, but it helps the support staff brush up on a missed name.

Other ideas for providing affirmation include holding a banquet at the end of the year to honor the peer leaders, recommending them for honors such as *Who's Who in American Colleges and Universities*, remembering birthdays and recognizing significant achievements with bulletin board announcements, thanking peer leaders on a personal basis for jobs well done, or hosting special meals throughout the semester such as an international food tasting party. Giving gifts of plants or mugs and water bottles with the college or program logo also demonstrates appreciation. Further, these gifts can be "teachable" if they are imprinted with the program's key goal or mission statement. Some campuses reward peer leaders by allowing them to register early for classes or move into the residence halls prior to the regular students. Staff members can also affirm peer leaders by treating them as equals and giving them their full attention when they have a need. Another way to do this is to encourage staff outside the department or program to recognize peer leader contributions. The president and chief academic and chief student affairs officers should be invited to attend peer leader training and recognition functions so that by their presence and their words they express the importance of student leaders for the whole institution.

At Southwest Missouri State University an appreciation outing is held for peer leaders, and the program coordinator writes a letter of thanks to each one stressing the importance of the leadership role he or she provides in the program. Students also receive one credit hour for attending training classes. Initially the student pays for the class, but the money is reimbursed halfway through the semester if the student has not withdrawn from the course. Showing appreciation and offering financial and academic incentives motivate peer leaders to return for a second year and help to recruit new peer leaders.

Another source of positive motivation is the creation of an open dialogue within and outside the office. This involves creating an environment where everyone feels comfortable expressing his or her ideas. One way this is done at Temple University is to have a box where peer leaders anonymously place concerns for the support staff to read. A supervisor's availability and openness are key in creating a climate of trust. Some strategies for creating and maintaining a dialogic climate are listed below.

Providing a Rationale for Decisions

Students often resent the authoritarian voice of the person who gives the orders; providing students with the rationale for decisions can short-circuit some of this resentment. Further, sharing reasons with students keeps them informed, makes them feel involved, and encourages them to complete the task more efficiently because they know the purpose. The bottom line is that this behavior communicates that students are seen as equals.

For example, Kean University recently changed the emphasis of its first-year seminar to a more academic focus with a letter grade. Initially, some peer leaders rebelled because they perceived this as a threat to the community-building goals of the course. When reasons were given that showed how this change would help disengaged students commit to their learning process, the peer leaders became supportive. They even began to generate their own ideas of how we can accomplish this new goal, creating a program involving oral, written, and research skills that is both academic and fun.

Giving Effective Feedback

« *Timing.* The use of proper timing when giving students feedback that is potentially conflictual keeps issues from escalating. Program coordinators should avoid initiating a potentially embarrassing discussion when they might be distracted by interruptions or when others are in earshot. At the same time, they will want to avoid confronting a student leader when he or she has just returned after failing a math exam or who is experiencing some other significant stress. The timing needs to be "right" for both the supervisor and the student to maximize the chances for a positive outcome.

« *"I" language.* One way to diffuse the emotional impact of negative feedback is to use "I" language. "I" language has the connotation of creating a nonjudgmental situation because it lacks the authoritarian use of words like "we" or "The Staff," which create a sense of superiority or exclusion that can be intimidating. It also avoids the judgmental connotation of "you did ..." that puts the student on the defensive in a way that invites a self-protecting statement that might only escalate a conflict.

» *The questioning approach.* Supervisors may adopt a questioning approach when giving negative feedback. This allows the student to have his or her say, and it gives the peer leader coordinator a fuller picture of the conflict because initial perceptions might be deceiving. Asking questions also encourages the student to work through problems by responding to appropriate questions. The dynamics at this stage of communication involve listening more than speaking and provide the student with an opportunity to disagree with or reframe the supervisor's opinion. But allowing the student to have greater control of the conversation might cloud the situation and put the supervisor on the defensive. Supervisors should keep the conversation focused on their questions, putting their own defensiveness aside. Ultimately, a questioning approach has the potential to teach critical reflection and to create greater student commitment to any resolution.

» *Being direct.* Considerations about timing, use of "I" language, and the questioning approach do not mean feedback should not be direct. Supervisors must be direct when providing feedback or students may be confused.

» *Balancing the negative with the positive.* Moreover, supervisors should be equally direct in providing positive feedback. Knowing what they are doing well makes it easier for students to accept negative feedback and motivates them to make the necessary changes. At Southwest Missouri State University, all peer leaders are evaluated half way through the semester by their instructor and by the students in their classes. Although the peer leader does not see the

evaluations, the peer leader coordinator sums up the evaluations in a way that ensures a constructive experience. Giving feedback that affirms the person positively gives the clear message that the criticism is not about the person, but about the situation.

» *Seeking clarification.* Many students, especially high achievers (who usually become student leaders), have a tendency to hear the negative louder than the positive. As people-pleasers, they are so conditioned to valuing the positive that anything negative might get blown out of proportion (Miller, 1996). For this reason, the supervisor should always ask students to summarize feedback so that he or she can clarify what has been said and what needs to happen next. High achievers may only hear the negative; summarizing and seeking clarification allows time for the conversation to be placed in perspective without undue distortion.

If an environment supporting open dialogue exists in the office, student leaders will be more likely to share problems and seek advice. This type of environment is essential for students who need to address a conflict with an instructor. A peer leader's supervisor helps balance the power in the instructor-peer relationship by coaching the student on what to say to a difficult instructor.

Creating a Climate of Professionalism

As discussed earlier, student peer leaders are persons-in-the-middle, causing them to experience role confusion or role ambiguity. The student may become so confident that he or she wants to run the program, or he or she may become lax in fulfilling responsibilities. A focus on professionalism can help peer leaders avoid these extremes. Kean University has stressed professionalism by giving our students business cards, which affirms their status as professionals. Some professors acknowledge the peer leaders as "professionals" by allowing them to give input into the grading process. The creation of a contract during training also emphasizes professionalism. If a student does not fulfill contractual responsibilities, he or she is dismissed.

Avoiding mixed messages for the students in the middle can alleviate confusion about how they should act and how students are to respond to them. This can be as simple as manipulating the physical and psychological space of the classroom. Meigan Kelly, a former peer leader at The University of South Carolina and now a supervisor at Temple University where the first-year seminar is an optional course, encourages the peer leader to have a seat with the instructor in the front of the room, giving the nonverbal message that the peer leader is a professional and that the two are a team.

Kean University is fortunate to have its program situated in the Center for New Students where a workspace, relaxation space, and study space have been established for the peer leaders. Each student is allowed one-hour preparation time before teaching a class. A quiet area of the office is set aside for this study and preparation. In this area the student is not asked to complete other tasks, reinforcing the importance of study and demonstrating a respect for privacy.

Students tend to become friends in peer leadership programs and will want to talk with each other about non-office issues. The Center for New Student's lunchroom gives peer leaders a place to hang out when they are not on duty. All other areas of the office are considered work areas, and the student is expected to behave professionally in these areas.

The following list provides additional strategies for encouraging professionalism among the peer leader staff:

« Make sure the student leader is informed of new information.

« Assign each leader a mailbox in a central office.

« Establish a sign-in and sign-out system to check peer leader attendance and call them to accountability.

« Post significant information on a bulletin board in a highly visible place, and establish the expectation that peer leaders check this board regularly.

« Provide peer leaders with a checklist of their responsibilities, reducing the chances that they will be overwhelmed by multiple responsibilities. (See Appendix B for a sample check list.)

« Publish a biweekly or monthly newsletter with reminders and program updates. This is also a good venue for recognizing staff members who have made important contributions to the program.

« Avoid overloading peer leaders with too many memos or announcements.

« Use technology to facilitate communication among the staff. Establish a group E-mail and/or voice mail list to distribute announcements and program updates. A listserv is also an excellent way for staff members to keep each other informed about things they have tried that have worked well, to ask for suggestions, and to discuss common concerns.

Friendships often develop between the supervisory staff and peer leaders because they are working closely with each other. However, boundaries must be set that ultimately are to the advantage of all parties. Failure to do so leads to a mixed message because peer leaders do not share equality with an instructor or with a supervisor. One way to clarify the message at Kean University has been for the supervisory staff to have their own lunch area, which helps to differentiate the roles in the office. In addition, supervisory staff and student leaders are on a first name basis in the office. This creates rapport, but it may become problematic when a peer leader uses a professional's first name in referring a student to that staff member. One way to resolve this has been to encourage an informality of names when interacting with each other in the office; however, students are instructed to use proper titles when introducing staff members or when taking phone messages or interacting with other staff and students outside the office.

> Avoiding mixed messages for the students in the middle can alleviate confusion about how they should act and how students are to respond to them.

Sometimes a peer leader and an instructor will become good friends. For the most part this is positive, but it can become negative when one covers for the other's failure to fulfill his or her responsibilities. The peer leader is sometimes the one who covers for the instructor. For this reason it becomes a worthwhile policy to limit to one semester a particular instructor-peer leader team. This policy encourages professionalism and provides the student with exposure to different teaching or interpersonal styles.

Professionalism involves creating an interdependent work environment. Program coordinators can encourage professionalism and foster interdependence by demonstrating a willingness to learn from the peer leaders. Peer leaders often see the program from multiple perspectives; encouraging their input and expressing how much it is valued not only affirms their role in the program but also provides valuable information for program assessment and development.

Learning interdependence and accepting personal limits are fundamental to leadership development, but these are difficult tasks for the peer leader who is developing confidence. Peer leaders want their students to succeed, but the reality is that not every student will share their concern or listen to their advice. An idealistic peer leader who is judging success by the immediate outcome and who wants to be liked by the students in the class might take the apparent rejection of his or her advice as a blow to the ego. The desire to make a difference in students' lives might also raise time management issues for enthusiastic peer leaders because of their willingness to over-extend themselves. A fast-paced society encourages this, making peer leaders more comfortable as doers rather than as empowerers who observe and point the way. At the same time instructors, who are part of support programs, are often generous with their time and energy. Part of the instructor's role is to mentor the student leader, but peer leaders should not expect that the instructor be their ever-present counselor whom they monopolize because they have found a listening ear. Program coordinators will need to help peer leaders recognize and respect their own personal limitations and the limitations of those with whom they work.

Moreover, role flexibility is part of the learning process. This is threatening for the peer leader who has excelled in one role and is asked to adapt to the changing roles of the team. With maturity comes the knowledge that context changes and that few situations fit into a cookie cutter mold. One also gains the ability to adapt to diverse situations (Perry, 1970).

This chapter has emphasized building rapport with peer leaders and building community while stressing the need for task completion and accountability. Group studies suggest that all groups need to find a balance between rapport and task completion if they are to reach their goals (Benne & Sheats, 1948; Lumsden & Lumsden, 1996). If one side of the equation is missing, the balance is thrown off; and the group accomplishes nothing or becomes explosive with tension. The support staff needs to avoid the extreme of the authoritarian leader who bosses students around and treats them like children, while at the same time the laissez-faire coordinator should not forget that peer leaders are still students, and he or she should not fail to provide them with enough direction.

The peer leader program has the potential to transform not only the students it serves but also the peer leaders who will remember the formative experiences gained in their leadership roles. Coordinators will also find that an emphasis on role clarification, training, and professionalism pays dividends for the institution in terms of a well-run and effective program and for the peer leader whose experiences have prepared him or her to assume a wide variety of leadership roles after leaving college.

References

Benne, K., & Sheats, P. (1948). Functional roles of group members. *The Journal of Social Issues, 4*, 41-49.

Blackburn-Smith, J., & Lembo, L. (1998). Managing student employees in a recruitment setting. *College and University, 74*(1), 6-15.

Donohue, W., & Kolt, R. (1992). *Managing interpersonal conflict*. Thousand Oaks, CA: Sage.

Habley, W. (1984). Student paraprofessionals in academic advising. In S. Ender, & R. Winston (Eds.), Students as paraprofessional staff. *New Directions for Student Services, 27* (pp. 37-49). San Francisco: Jossey-Bass.

Kouzes, J., & Posner, B. (1999). *Encouraging the heart: A leader's guide to rewarding and recognizing others*. San Francisco: Jossey-Bass.

Kurvink, K. (1993, March-April). "Contracting" as a motivational tool. *Journal of College Science Teaching*, 310-311.

Larson, C., & LaFasto, F. (1989). *Team work*. Thousand Oaks, CA: Sage.

Lumsden, G., & Lumsden, D. (1996). *Communicating with credibility and confidence*. Boston, MA: Wadsworth Publishing.

MacGregor, J. (Ed.). (1993). Student self-evaluation: Fostering reflective learning. *New Directions for Teaching and Learning, 56*. San Francisco: Jossey-Bass.

Miller, A. (1996). *The drama of the gifted child*. New York: Harper Collins.

Perry, W. (1970). *Forms of intellectual and ethical development in the college years*. New York: Holt, Rinehart, and Winston.

Schön, D. (1983). *The reflective practitioner*. New York: Basic Books.

CHAPTER 4

THE BUILDING BLOCKS OF THE PEER LEADER PROGRAM: RECRUITMENT, SELECTION, AND TRAINING

Mary Stuart Hunter and Misty M. Heath

The Importance of Recruitment, Selection, and Training

Business and industry, the armed forces, and higher education are just three of the many segments of society that have recognized the importance of effective leadership education, management training, and organizational development. High-powered consultants engage in lucrative speaking tours and write bestselling books on these topics. Corporations invest millions of dollars in recruitment and training for new employees. The Unites States Armed Forces requires extensive boot camps for new soldiers prior to service. Colleges and universities have created entire majors and degree programs centered on training issues in schools of business administration. Higher educators administering peer leader programs have also recognized that effective recruitment, selection, and training efforts are essential to the success of any meaningful program. These necessary components of a peer leader program lay the foundation upon which the program's structure is built and upon which its goals and objectives are attained. As reported in Chapter 5, undergraduate peer leaders are found in a variety of settings in higher education (e.g., first-year seminars, residence halls, academic advising, tutoring centers, counseling centers). Although the specific program setting will determine the specific approaches used in recruitment, selection, and training, many elements are generic enough to be applicable to a variety of programs. This chapter will present pertinent issues and themes related to these three aspects of peer leader programs and will offer practical and concrete suggestions for developing, implementing, and assessing these processes.

In 1999, Suzanne Hamid and Jayson VanHook of Lee University administered a survey designed to increase understanding of issues related to peer leader recruitment, selection, and training in first-year seminar programs. The survey was sent to approximately 81 institutions, which had indicated on the National Survey of First-Year Seminar Programs (National Resource Center for The First-Year Experience and Students in Transition, 1997) that undergraduate students were involved with instruction in first-year seminars. Of those 81, 40 institutions responded. The respondents represented a wide variety of institutional types ranging from small, private colleges to large, research universities. Many of the suggestions and ideas presented in this chapter are based on the responses to the survey and are drawn from presentations at The First-Year Experience Conferences sponsored by the National Resource Center for The

First-Year Experience and Students in Transition at the University of South Carolina. Additionally, the authors' experiences with peer leader programs in first-year seminars at the University of South Carolina and Florida State University serve as background for many of the examples shared. While many of the suggestions presented in this chapter are applicable to a wide range of peer leader programs, much of the research and experience upon which this chapter is based is in the area of the first-year seminar. As a result, some of the discussion here is specifically relevant to this type of program.

Recruitment

Peer Leader Characteristics / Criteria

When Alice in her adventures in Wonderland asks of the Cheshire Cat, "Would you tell me, please, which way I ought to go from here?", the Cat responds, "That depends a good deal on where you want to get to" (Carroll, 1990, p. 78). So, too, a vigorous recruitment program begins with the end in mind. Before beginning recruitment, selection, or training, a first imperative is to spend time and effort on initial planning. Knowing "where one wants to go" will certainly aid in getting there. Before recruitment efforts begin, consideration should be given to the characteristics sought in the students who will serve as peer leaders. These characteristics should reflect the goals of the program and the expectations the program director has of the students who will serve as peer leaders. The process of developing a job description or a list of potential roles for peer leaders can aid in identifying desirable characteristics. Knowing what characteristics are desirable will make it easier to recruit and select appropriate peer leaders.

During job description development, the criteria for the selection process may also be created. In order for a successful recruitment process to unfold, stated qualifications should be established so they can be communicated throughout the recruitment and selection process. The demands on students before, during, and following their experience as peer leaders should be reflected in the established guidelines. The specific criteria for peer leaders will depend on the institutionally specific program goals. Based on responses in the 1999 survey (Hamid & VanHook, 1999), the following are topics most commonly addressed when establishing the peer leader criteria:

Grade point average (GPA). Will a minimum grade point average be set? If peer leaders are intended to serve as role models for the first-year students, should academic success be a key selection criterion? What is a reasonable standard to set that will ensure selection of peer leaders who are academic role models yet is not set so high that it limits the field of potential applicants? Will cumulative grade point average determine qualification, or will allowances be made for recent academic success in students who had a difficult academic beginning as first-year students? If a key role of peer leaders is to relate to students at a variety of achievement levels, should a high GPA be used as criteria or should peer leaders with a variety of academic experiences be considered?

Campus involvement and leadership. Involvement on campus is a factor affecting student retention (Astin, 1984). If one of the goals or intended outcomes of a first-year seminar program is to have a positive influence on the retention of students, should the peer leaders model involvement in campus life? Is demonstrated leadership on campus a desired criterion for peer leaders? If so, how will leadership and involvement be defined and measured?

Program experience. Is it desirable for peer leaders to have experience with the program from the "receiving end"? For example, should peer leaders in residence halls for first-year students have themselves lived in residence halls as first-year students? Given that first-year seminars are elective courses on many campuses, it is entirely possible for students who meet the qualifications to become peer leaders without having actually enrolled in first-year seminars during their first year. To what extent will requiring previous experience with the program limit or restrict the pool of qualified students?

Student classification. When considering peer leader qualifications, program directors should determine what level or classification of student they require to fill program goals and needs. At least the following questions should be considered: What level or length of experience is desirable for the peer leaders? Should peer leaders only be juniors or seniors, or should sophomores also be eligible? In addition, should transfer students be considered? How long should a student be at a particular institution before becoming eligible to become a peer leader (if previous participation in the program is not required)?

Major or department. During initial planning for the program's recruitment and selection efforts, one should consider what type of student will most effectively further the goals of the program. The following questions should be considered: Does a student's academic major or academic concentration matter in his or her role as a peer leader? Is it desirable for the peer leader program to have a group of peer leaders representing a variety of disciplines?

Other criteria. Do other program attributes suggest specific characteristics required in peer leaders? If so, what are they? When determining specific qualifications and responsibilities of the peer leaders, one should keep in mind unique institutional cultures, student needs, and program characteristics. In doing so, program staff will be establishing clear and specific criteria for their peer leaders, which should result in a qualified, dynamic group of students ready to be trained to serve the program and other students.

Incentives

In addition to composing a job description for peer leaders, one should also consider what, if any, incentive(s) serving as a peer leader might offer. Is this a volunteer position? Or will the students be paid for their time and efforts? Is there an option to gain course credit for serving as a peer leader? Incentives may take the form of specific rewards and compensation such as tuition reimbursement, money for books and supplies, payment, academic credit, scholarships, as well as more simple rewards in the form of certificates, t-shirts, social functions, or letters of commendation and appreciation. Another incentive to consider is whether this experience will aid the peer leaders in reaching their own educational and vocational goals. Potential benefits and common outcomes of the peer leader experience may be stressed in the recruitment process. A quality peer leader program can facilitate growth and development in those who serve as peer leaders in a variety of ways such as providing a substantial leadership opportunity, providing college-level teaching experience, offering exposure to a diverse population of students, and providing a setting in which peer leaders can assess and reflect upon their own development and collegiate experience. By planning ahead and considering what incentives will attract the best possible students to the program (given program budget and resource limitations), a program administrator will be able to gain

> Another incentive to consider is whether this experience will aid the peer leaders in reaching their own educational and vocational goals. Potential benefits and common outcomes of the peer leader experience may be stressed in the recruitment process.

insight into how best to recruit and select the most qualified peer leaders.

Southwest Missouri State University offers one example of an incentive plan, which includes peer leader enrollment in a one-semester for-credit course. At the beginning of the semester, these students pay tuition for this course. However, they are reimbursed for the course tuition at midterm. The intent is to increase the likelihood of the students' commitment to the course and the program; they are not required to cover the cost for the course if they fulfill their commitment (Casady, 1999).

Application Content

Early in the recruitment planning process, decisions should be made regarding the content of the application materials. The application packet should reflect the criteria and desired characteristics established for peer leaders. A variety of possibilities exist, with the following representing some of the most commonly reported components (Hamid & VanHook, 1999):

« *Demographic/contact information.* Most basic to any application is demographic information about the applicant. It should include the student's name, student identification number, both the campus and permanent addresses, phone number, e-mail address, classification, and grade point average. Consider including any additional information, such as gender or ethnic background, (within legal parameters) that will facilitate the selection process and will allow for easy communication with the applicants.

« *Essay.* Many programs will include an essay as a key element of the application, which typically separates the mildly interested applicants from those who have a keen desire to perform the duties and responsibilities of a peer leader. Many essays ask students to write about the reasons they are interested in becoming peer leaders, what they can contribute to the program, and what qualities they possess that would make them effective peer leaders. An essay requirement in an application packet also offers the added dimension of illustrating the student's writing skills and abilities, which can serve as another way to assess the student's intellectual ability, beyond that measured by the grade point average.

« *Recommendations and references.* As with any "job selection" process, references and recommendations can be valuable. The information gained through this process can provide a perspective on the applicant that he or she cannot provide. Recommendations or references can take the form of letters of support, a recommendation form, or simply contact information to be used by those responsible for the selection. Careful thought should be given to what information is desired and what form it should take. Guidelines for acceptable references should be clearly articulated on the application in order to yield appropriate information.

« *Transcript.* If a minimum grade point average and or class standing is a stated criteria for peer leader selection, an official transcript as part of the application packet will assist in the selection process and ease the work load of those administering the selection.

Sample applications are in Appendix A.

Avenues for Recruitment

Once the qualifications and criteria have been developed, recruitment efforts can begin. When devising the recruitment plan, given the target peer leader audience based on the position criteria, only time and budget limit potential avenues for recruitment. Successful recruitment calls for creative measures; however, the following outlines some of the more traditional tactics for recruitment.

Nominations. Perhaps the most effective method of recruitment involving the entire campus community is a nomination process. The solicitation of outstanding students draws attention to the peer leader program and gives program administrators the opportunity to communicate the high standards of the seminar program to a variety of campus constituents. An obvious target group from which to solicit nominations are the program faculty/staff members themselves. These faculty and staff are committed to the program by virtue of the fact that they are teaching in or administering the program. They may recall former students who were successful in their classes, who benefited from the program themselves, and who would have an interest in collaborating to create a similar experience for new students. Faculty members generally have as much contact with students as any other individuals on campus and may thus be invaluable resources for recruitment.

For peer leader programs already in existence, current and former peer leaders can also be invited to submit nominations. As students themselves, they may know others who would be effective peer leaders and who would have an interest in the experience. In addition, students should be invited to nominate themselves. Many students may be searching for a significant leadership experience. Self-selecting through a self-nomination process requires a great deal of initiative and should be made possible for these highly motivated students.

Application availability. Applications should be made easily accessible. Upon nomination, applications should be sent promptly to those nominated. At the same time, a letter of appreciation to the nominators will both acknowledge the nomination and provide an opportunity for additional campus-wide positive public relations for the program. Printed applications can be made available at the program office and elsewhere on campus where such information and materials are normally distributed. Applications may also be made available on the World Wide Web.

Advertising on campus. Many campuses have a multitude of information dissemination vehicles available for institutionally sponsored programs and events such as student newspapers and student-managed broadcast media. An organized and well-planned advertising blitz can quickly get the word out about the application process, bringing attention to the seminar program and the peer leader component.

Student newspapers offer several possibilities for campus information dissemination, both at a cost to the program and for free. A feature article or news story timed to appear during the recruitment process is an excellent way to provide good public relations for the program in general as well as specific information on the peer leader recruitment process. To achieve this, start early, well before the recruitment process kicks off. If a feature article or news story does not materialize, paid advertising space may be available.

Many campuses have broadcast media (e.g., campus radio stations, television stations, cable networks) that post public service and campus activity announcements. Sending a brief announcement to the general managers or advertising directors requesting that they post an announcement about the recruitment process can prove effective if done well in advance of the desired broadcast dates.

Traditional forms of advertising to student audiences include posters, signs, and table tents. Eye-catching and professional-looking advertising pieces placed strategically around campus can reach students and inform them of the recruitment process. Consider strategic locations on campus frequented by students who would make good peer leaders. Signs and posters placed in such locations as student government offices and honors program offices can prove fruitful. Table tents on the tables in dining halls and snack bars can advertise the recruitment process and provide information for many students, as all students eat at one time or another.

Student organizations. Announcements made at the meetings of key student organizations can be a very useful avenue of information dissemination, especially if demonstrated student leadership is one of the criteria for peer leader selection. Current or former peer leaders can be enlisted to make these announcements, or letters can be sent to organization presidents requesting that announcements be made.

Information meetings. Another viable method to recruit peer leaders on campus is to hold several information sessions. These sessions should be well advertised and presented at convenient times for students, with a variety of days and times offered. A number of things may be accomplished during these meetings. First, interested students and program administrators can have an opportunity to meet each other. The position responsibilities can be reviewed as well as application criteria and application deadlines. During these sessions, past and current peer leaders can "sell" the peer leader experience as well as offer suggestions, success stories, and the challenges and benefits of the peer leader experience. Finally, applications can be distributed to interested students at these sessions.

Other avenues for recruitment. When determining how best to market and recruit, program directors must keep in mind their particular institution's culture. Is it a primarily residential campus? If so, then residence halls and resident advisors may be a productive target audience. Likewise, flyers on windshields or signs in parking lots and public transit stops can effectively reach students at commuter campuses. Using institutional technology is also a viable and inexpensive means for recruitment. By posting messages on listservs, web sites, and discussion lists, program administrators can draw even more attention to the program.

A Well-planned Recruitment Effort

As outlined, many avenues for recruitment are available, and many more can be conceived and developed. Advanced planning can assist program administrators in developing a plan that wisely uses the limited funds available for program support and development. Starting early and developing a timeline for recruitment efforts can also help ensure a coordinated recruitment process. (The recruitment timeline used at the University of South Carolina is provided in Appendix A.) Without an effective recruitment process, a peer leader program will have greater difficulty achieving the potential positive outcomes and providing the growth experience for both first-year students and peer leaders themselves. In short, without an effective recruitment process, a quality peer leader program cannot exist.

Selection

Selection criteria that are carefully and consciously formulated and communicated during the recruitment phase can provide a basis for a smooth selection process. Yet, following a productive and successful recruitment process, a more difficult challenge faces program administrators—peer leader selection. A rushed or poorly executed selection process opens up the opportunity for a bumpy road during the academic term when the peer leaders take on their position responsibilities. Conversely, a thorough and rigorous selection process can pave the way for a smoothly implemented program with peer

> . . .group interviews can be less time consuming and put less strain on limited resources than individual interviews, especially for large programs supporting 100 peer leaders or more.

leaders fulfilling their roles in productive and educationally sound ways. As with a solid foundation for a house or other building, the selection of the individuals who will serve the program as peer leaders must be considered fundamental to building a successful program.

Composing a Selection Committee

Although at times cumbersome, a selection committee of several individuals can be more effective than a single individual in making the sometimes-difficult decisions in selection, while increasing the likelihood of fairness and consistency. In addition, sharing responsibility and accountability may be liberating for program administrators. Including individuals with differing perspectives and backgrounds can create rich discussions and lead to better selection decisions. In addition to the program administrator, selection committee members may include program support staff, current peer leaders or student leaders on campus, and faculty or staff with no connection to the program. Individuals invited to serve on the selection committee should be open-minded, conscientious, and have a full understanding of the goals and objectives of the peer leader program. The size of the applicant pool and the number of positions available will determine the amount of time demanded of the selection committee. The program administrator should communicate an estimate of the necessary time commitment to the potential members when forming the committee.

Application Review

The first step in the selection process involves a review of the applications. As each application is received, it should first be checked to confirm that the form is complete and that the applicant meets the minimum qualifications. When the application deadline passes and the pool of complete applications is compiled, the review can begin. If the volume of applications is manageable, the initial review process can be accomplished as a group with the entire committee reviewing each application. If, however, the size of the applicant pool is large, a process of dividing the applications into smaller groups for initial review may be advisable.

Interviews

Many comprehensive selection processes include an interview. Some programs will conduct individual interviews; others will use group interviews. A number of methods can be employed when organizing interviews. If interviews are to be incorporated into the selection process, the interview component should reflect specific goals and must be well planned, with careful decisions made about how the interview will be structured.

When planning individual interviews, there are a number of issues to consider. First, who will conduct the interviews? In some programs, past or current peer leaders conduct the interviews, while in others the program director or selection committee conducts the interviews. Many incorporate a combination of program staff, the director, current peer leaders, instructors, and others. Next, one should consider the format for the interview. Will the questions be predetermined and the same set of questions asked of all applicants or will there be some variability depending on the individual student and his or her application? In addition, how much time is needed to reach a fair assessment of the student's qualifications without straining valuable time and resources? How will the interviews be evaluated and how will those involved be able to provide feedback and recommendations regarding the applicant's status? All of these questions should be weighed before the interviews begin.

Many programs opt to facilitate a group interview process. There are a number of reasons why a group interview can be beneficial. First, group interviews can be less time consuming and put less strain on limited resources than individual interviews, especially for large programs supporting 100 peer leaders or more. In addition, a group interview can yield valuable information regarding a student's ability to relate to people, listen, perform tasks, think critically, respect differences, and work in a group. In considering a group interview, one should take into account the duration of the interviews, the format to be used, the number of students to involve in each group interview, and how evaluation of the applicants will be structured.

Whether an individual or group interview is conducted, these forums can provide insight into the individual applicant's interpersonal communication skills. Though time consuming, interviews can allow face-to-face interaction between the applicant and selection committee which, in turn, can provide valuable information to the applicant and the program director not possible without the interview experience.

Selection Issues

A number of issues may arise during the selection process. The total number of peer leader positions available will, of course, affect the selection process. Selecting from a large pool of applicants for a limited number of positions can be challenging, but it can also help to raise the quality level of peer leaders. Demographic needs specific to the program may also influence the selection process. For example, desired race and gender representation can affect peer leader selection. Several institutions reported in the 1999 survey that many fewer males than females apply for peer leader positions (Hamid & VanHook, 1999). In such situations, if it is desirable to have an increased number of males in the peer leader roles, will selection criteria be altered for males? Do ethnic background goals exist for the program that need to be met? Will special considerations be made in order to involve students of underrepresented groups?

Academic major can also be a stratification need if programs are discipline-specific. This is frequently seen in academic advising and first-year seminar programs. If faculty members and staff are active in the recruitment and nomination process, there may be students who have been highly recommended by them who do not meet stated criteria. In some cases faculty members or staff will recruit specific students with whom they wish to teach or advise who will fall short of the selection criteria. Will such students be accepted into the program? Other unforeseen issues may also arise. For example, will deadlines be strictly enforced? It may be that an outstanding application arrives after the deadline. Such demographic and staffing needs are best determined prior to review of individual applications, so as not to affect selection more than necessary. In any case, program administrators may want to consult the campus legal office to ensure that any changes made during the selection process meet legal requirements.

Training

Once the process of selecting an outstanding group of peer leaders has been accomplished, another fundamental process must begin: providing a training experience that is informational, inspirational, and developmental. Preparing peer leaders for what to expect in their new roles with new responsibilities can be a complex task, but nevertheless, it is an essential one. Training is a critical component of an effective peer leader program; in fact, 100% of the 40 responding institutions in the 1999 survey indicated that they provide some form of training for peer leaders (Hamid & VanHook, 1999). Training can take many forms, but two prevalent forms of training are a credit-bearing academic course taken prior to or concurrent with the peer leader experience and a preparation workshop. The content and process can be similar for these two formats with adjustments made to fit the schedule and to meet the goals of the training. Following is a discussion of the issues involved in peer leader training.

Training Process

Training should be designed to inform and inspire at the same time it prepares newly selected peer leaders for their new role. A four-phase model for training of first-year seminar instructors (Gardner, 1981), developed at the University of South Carolina and replicated at hundreds of institutions, is highly adaptable and can serve as a useful framework for training peer leaders in a variety of settings. Gardner's four phases include: (a) developing a sense of community and building group trust, (b) identifying the needs and characteristics of learners, (c) identifying and developing resources to address the needs of the learners, and (d) developing strategies for incorporating workshop content and outcomes in other settings. Each of these stages is described in more detail below:

« *Phase 1: Developing a sense of community and building group trust.* During this first phase, ice breaker activities and group building exercises allow peer leaders who have arrived at the training workshop as strangers to become acquainted with one another, make new friends, discover common interests, and begin the process of becoming a cohesive group. This community-building phase provides the foundation for the creation of an environment that will maximize learning during the remainder of the workshop. If students are comfortable in a new environment with a new group of people (i.e. the workshop environment), they are more likely to learn from the opinions, ideas, content, and activities presented during the workshop.

« *Phase 2: Identifying the needs and characteristics of learners.* In Phase 2, peer leaders can be guided through experiences that allow them to identify their potential roles as peer leaders and the knowledge and characteristics that are necessary for them to be effective in these roles. Common situations as well as common problems encountered by peer leaders can be presented, giving new peer leaders a sense of what is to come. A focus on the needs and characteristics of the students they will serve during the peer leader experience can also be useful. Some examples of these kinds of activities include discussions or presentations on how to handle disruptive or problem students, how to address issues regarding the program staff/instructor-peer leader relationship and how to encourage active student involvement in the program. Individuals can then assess what they need to learn in order to prepare for their role.

« *Phase 3: Identifying and developing resources to address the needs of the learners.* The third phase follows logically from Phase 2 in that once the characteristics, knowledge, and roles are identified, a process of identifying what needs to be learned is undertaken. Support resources are identified from a variety of sources—the knowledge and skills of the individuals in the workshop, those of the training leaders, the campus-at-large, and the local community. To help with this phase, many workshops will include a panel of former peer leaders to share their experiences with workshop participants.

« *Phase 4: Developing strategies for incorporating workshop content and outcomes in other settings.* The final phase encourages participants to reflect on what they have learned and to consider how they might use what they have learned in their work as peer leaders. This bridging or transition phase will continue long after the initial training workshop concludes as peer leaders draw on the workshop experience in planning for their role as peer leaders and then as they actually begin to experience peer leadership.

Workshop Content

The workshop content should reflect the goals of the program as well as what is to be expected of the peer leaders. When considering the training process, one should ask, "How can we provide a learning environment for new peer leaders during the training that re-creates the experience that occurs during the actual program?" Trainers at Franklin College have found that returning peer leaders can be use to provide effective training (Priser, Johnson, & McCarthy, 1999, p. 73). Such training workshops also allow peer leaders to make connections with other peer leaders they may not meet otherwise and help build peer leaders' confidence in their ability to be effective in new roles. In fact, Ender and Newton (2000) state, "For effective training to occur, group members must feel comfortable with one another and know that personal risk-taking and sharing is acceptable and encouraged" (p. 6). The following are other issues to consider or topics and activities to address when planning and implementing peer leader training.

History/goals of program. For peer leaders to effectively serve their students, they must first be introduced to and understand the role the program plays in the college experience. The new peer leaders should understand the program's impact on student retention, the philosophy and history of the program, as well as program goals. Students may also be interested in knowing the history of the peer leader program and its evolution at their particular institution.

Leadership education. The experience students have during training for their roles as peer leaders can develop skills and abilities transferable to other settings and experiences. The Leadership in Action program at Champlain College includes a course for peer leaders designed to do more than simply train peer leaders. Its added intent is to help students acquire an appreciation for the complexities of leadership (Goldsweig, 1999). Topics in the course include the nature and qualities of leadership, ethics and values, power, and leadership styles.

Student development theory. A working knowledge of basic student development theories, such as Arthur Chickering's theory of identity development (1969, 1993) or William Perry's theory of intellectual and ethical development (1968), can be helpful in the peer leader training experience. First, by understanding student development theory, program administrators can devise a training program they consider appropriate to the peer leaders' level of development and their needs as students. Secondly, by introducing student development theory to peer leaders, they may gain a deeper understanding of the students they will be serving and how they, as peer leaders, can aid in their students' development. Peer leaders apply student development theory to daily experiences as guided by their course facilitator in Montana State University's General Studies first-year seminar course (Orazem, Buchanan, & Roller, 1998). Knowledge of student development theory will also allow the peer leaders to reflect on their own growth since their first year in college—how the significant people who were a part of their first year, including their peer leader, may have aided in their personal development.

First-year transition issues. One benefit of peer leaders is their ability to provide perspectives and anecdotes to students and instructors on common first-year student transition issues. Peer leaders are generally better able to understand common adjustment problems and fears faced by many new students—such as homesickness, drinking, academic issues, roommate problems, time and financial management, social adjustment, and peer pressure—than are faculty and staff members. Peer leaders need to know, however, that while their experience and their ability to relate to students can greatly benefit students, every student experience is different. What may have worked for them in the past will not work for every one of their own students. Introducing peer leaders to common transition issues supplements their own experiences with a more general understanding of the challenges facing first-year students.

During the training program at Lee University, students take a close look at the first-year class profile using Cooperative Institutional Research Program (CIRP) data (Hamid & VanHook, 1999). This provides students an understanding of the demographics of their first-year class, as well as their ability levels, interests, fears, needs, and experiences. By introducing these data to peer leaders, they gain a broader perspective on first-year students.

Course content. For peer leader programs that involve instruction, specific course content can be covered during the training sessions. The subtitle of Neal A. Whitman's 1988 ASHE-ERIC Higher Education Report, "To Teach is to Learn Twice," supports the value and power of peer teaching. Not only will the students in a class team-taught by peer leaders learn, but the peers also will learn or re-learn the content that they teach.

Program planners may want to present sample lessons, activities, and interventions that have been helpful in presenting common information or ideas. In a first-year seminar, these may be activities on library skill development, academic integrity, problem solving, building rapport with students and instructor, diversity, alcohol and other drug use and abuse, leading a group, learning styles, values clarification, study skills, effective communication, career development, syllabus planning, case studies, icebreakers, campus resources, and providing closure. Given the duration of the training and available time for activities, one may want to consider developing a comprehensive notebook or packet that can serve as a resource for the leaders throughout the semester. Soliciting feedback from the current peer leaders and incorporating their suggestions can strengthen this resource notebook for future leaders.

An exemplary training activity for first-year seminars occurs at Radford University, where students are given an opportunity to develop their own lesson plans which they then practice teaching (Hamid & VanHook, 1999). This way, students will have an opportunity for a "trial run" to develop a lesson on a specific topic, present it to a group, and receive feedback on how well they did. This also allows students to begin to identify their strengths as peer leaders as well as areas they may need to improve.

Role Definition

A common issue to address during training is role definition (Hamid & VanHook, 1999). Before students begin their position, they should first know what specific roles they will assume. These roles will vary from institution to institution, from program to program. Role definition is perhaps the most difficult issue to address for first-year seminar programs, due to the variability of responsibilities, personalities, goals of instructors and peer leaders, needs of students, and so on. Therefore, it is important to include the instructor participation during this phase of training, so each team can develop their own norms and expectations. The University of South Carolina University 101 program facilitates team-building workshops where peer leaders and instructors come together in the spring prior to teaching in the fall (see Appendix C for workshop agenda). One activity included in these workshops requires the teams to devise a strategy for teaching one of the required course areas referred to as "skills for living." The teams then prepare a 30-minute lesson plan. This allows the peer leaders and

> ...by introducing student development theory to peer leaders, they may gain a deeper understanding of the students they will be serving and how they, as peer leaders, can aid in their students' development.

the instructors an opportunity to brainstorm together and plan how they can divide the labor when planning the syllabus and class lessons.

During this important role-defining stage, the general responsibilities of the position should be reiterated to ensure student understanding and commitment. Many institutions use a peer leader contract toward this aim. By signing a contract, students signify their understanding of their roles and responsibilities to the seminar program and that they knowingly accept this responsibility. (See Appendix A for sample contracts—Lee University and Kean University offer good examples.)

Workshop Facilitators

Ideally, workshop leaders should include individuals who are both familiar with the first-year seminar program and the peer leader component of the program and those who possess effective facilitation skills. As Staley argues (1999), "In training faculty to teach the first-year seminar, there is perhaps no variable more important than the training facilitator" (p. 67). This also holds true for the training of other types of peer leaders. Staley continues:

> Obviously, trainers must have well-cultivated communication skills. However, effective training involves more than the ability to deliver a coherent and interesting lecture. Training at its best involves managing lively discussion generated by knowledgeable participants with diverse opinions as well as processing experiential exercises designed to engage and enlighten. Successful facilitators *relate* well to individual trainees and to the group as a whole, and they can help trainees *relate* to each other and to the material being discussed. (p. 68)

Having a team, rather than a single individual, charged with designing and facilitating the

workshop program information is usually desirable. Co-facilitation is an effective way to present experiential activities and exercises, because multiple trainers may be able "to cover skill sets outside [the program administrator's] experience" (Ender & Newton, 2000, p. 5). The team may consist of the program director, outside consultants, faculty, past and present peer leaders, or whoever else will provide the best possible training for the students. Also, the process of collaboration and emphasis on teamwork involved in co-facilitation model skills desired of peer leaders. Moreover, bringing in people from other areas may add credibility to the training and to the program (Ender & Newton, 2000).

Training Logistics

Although the content and process of training is important, the logistical planning of training workshops should also be given special consideration. Determining dates and times to accommodate all student schedules can be a challenging task. Yet, if attendance at the training workshop is not possible for all of the newly selected peer leaders, then the recruitment and selection process has been for naught. Select a time when students can attend, with the full knowledge that the time may not be what the program administrators or faculty members would desire. Decisions need to be made as to the duration of the workshop(s), keeping in mind the following questions: How much time will be needed to accomplish the desired outcomes? Can all objectives be accomplished in one workshop or will more than one workshop be required? Will the workshop need to be offered more than once to accommodate personal schedules and the number of peer leaders in the program? As Ender and Newton (2000) suggest, "Determining what learning outcomes and skill development you wish to accomplish will assist you as you decide on the length, duration, and format of training, as well as the need for in-service follow-up" (p. 4).

The physical setting of the workshop also plays an important role in the success of the training. Although most institutions (29 of the 40) participating in the 1999 survey reported that training took place on campus, others chose a retreat setting such as a state park or camp facility (Hamid & VanHook, 1999). When considering a potential training location, one should choose a location with ample parking that is easy to find and accessible to all. To ensure the most appropriate environment for learning and open communication, coordinators should make sure that the facility has adequate and controllable heating and air conditioning, cheerful lighting, and comfortable seating adaptable to small group work (Hunter & Cuseo, 1999).

Ongoing Training and Support

There is an important connection between the initial workshop experience and ongoing support and training. Ongoing contact is key to the personal growth and development of the peer leaders. Continued contact with the peer leaders can also help maintain a quality program. Many campuses incorporate a structured, ongoing connection with the peer leaders through periodically scheduled meetings for processing the experiences, or through a credit-bearing academic course taken concurrently with their peer leader experience. Sample syllabi for such courses can be found in Appendix A. Other campuses offer less formal ongoing support through the maintenance of a peer leader electronic listserv.

Other Program Considerations

Peer Instructor Teams

Matching. An important element in the potential for success in the peer leader experience is a suitable peer-instructor match. From the peer leader perspective, the compatibility of an instructor and peer is perhaps the most critical element in a successful experience. The 1999 survey revealed no one, best formula for

matching peer leaders with their instructors; however, the following details the most commonly used methods:

« *Program director/committee match.* This is perhaps the least time consuming and bureaucratic method to use when matching instructors with peer leaders. At both Avila College and Lee University, efforts are made to match returning peer leaders with new instructors and returning instructors are matched with new peer leaders whenever possible (Hamid & VanHook, 1999).

« *Student/instructor choice.* This method allows students and instructors to have some input into the match.

« *Time availability or by major.* Depending on the program structure and class times, this method may be more efficient in matching instructors and peer leaders.

No matter what pairing method or combination of methods is used, and depending on the size of the program, it is best to consider which matched pair will provide the best possible learning experience for the peer leader, instructor, and most of all, the first-year seminar students.

Team development. After matches are made, it is also desirable to have some structured time for instructors and peer leaders to work together before their team-teaching experience. At Southwest Missouri State University, peer leaders and instructors have a number of opportunities to interact prior to the beginning of the semester. They are required to meet to develop the course syllabus, design and complete a form regarding teacher and peer leader expectations, and establish a weekly meeting time for the entire semester (Casady, 1999). While a joint training workshop is not always possible (but encouraged), some opportunity for combined training and team development is important. In the 1999 survey, half of the respondents (20 of the 40) indicated that some or all of their program training involved both peer leaders and instructors together. One example is Russell Sage College, where peer leaders have a five-day training workshop with their faculty mentor (Hamid & VanHook, 1999). In order to facilitate an effective team approach to teaching the first-year seminar, New Mexico State University instituted a faculty/staff and peer educator training model that includes four key elements: (a) defining the role of the team, (b) analyzing teaching and learning styles of the team, (c) developing classroom co-facilitation skills, and (d) improving communication skills (Brown & Cook, 1999).

One team-building exercise developed at Hardin-Simmons University engages team members in an activity designed to encourage discussion about effective teamwork (Lybrand & Kieffer, 1999). The exercise requires small teaching teams to construct an object, in a very limited amount of time, that represents an ideal teaching team using only common office supplies (paper clips, index cards, tape, rubber bands, stick-on notes, string, etc). Each team member has a prescribed role (e.g., materials acquisition, builder, and communicator). The team must then describe to the larger training group, in 10 words or less, what the object represents. The exercise requires teamwork and makes the team members distill into very few words the essence of teamwork—and it is fun. While combined training workshops may not be possible at all institutions, they do allow for rich dialogue and team development to occur long before instructional teams ever enter the classroom.

Evaluation and Assessment

Summative evaluation immediately following training programs and prior to the peer leader experience can be very useful. End-of-workshop evaluations can provide information about which segments of the training workshops worked well and which ones did not. Areas not well received can be redesigned for future workshops. Critical content areas can be assessed, and evaluations of these areas may aid in determining where additional support and information is needed as the students begin their roles as peer leaders. Formative evaluation and assessment during the peer leader experience can also assist program administrators in trouble-shooting problem areas at the time and in adapting the program in the future. It is also useful for program planners to assess the training program at the conclusion of the peer leader experience, as a reflection on what would have been useful to the peer leaders during their experience. If an academic course for peer leaders is a part of the program, the final exam can be structured in such a way as to have students reflect on their entire peer leader experience, asking them to evaluate specific aspects of the program and their personal experience and to make recommendations to program administrators for program improvement.

Outcomes

Empirical research on the outcomes and effectiveness of peer leader recruitment, selection, and training is virtually non-existent. Anecdotal evidence, however, abounds and is used extensively in evaluation, assessment, and program refinement. Program administrators consciously or unconsciously review their success in the recruitment and selection process each year as the newly selected cohort takes form. Effective efforts are noted, and ideas for improvement are incorporated into future planning efforts. The effectiveness of training is often measured by responses on written evaluation forms for training workshops and on final exam reflections for peer leader courses. Program administrators often measure the effectiveness of the selection and training by how well the peer leaders serve in their roles and by how smoothly the program runs. Through peer leader and program administrator assessment, potential outcomes can focus on the effects of peer leader programs on the students served, on the peer leaders themselves, on the program in which the peer leaders serve, and on the institution as a whole.

Summary and Recommendations

Providing a solid foundation through recruitment, selection, and training is fundamental to ensuring the potential effectiveness of any program. These important preliminary phases, often considered unimportant, are perhaps paramount to a program's potential to succeed and thrive. This chapter has presented pertinent issues and offered practical and concrete suggestions for developing and implementing the recruitment, selection and training of peer leaders. The following recommendations summarize key elements of effective efforts.

1. Consider the importance placed on recruitment and training in the corporate and government worlds as evidenced by the dedication of financial resources. Use this as a guide when allocating budgetary resources in peer leader programs.

2. Develop and articulate clear program goals and objectives before initiating the recruitment and selection of peer leaders.

3. Disseminate the goals, objectives, and benefits of the program widely to inform and to publicize the peer leader component of the program.

4. Clearly describe peer leader job duties, responsibilities, and anticipated benefits in a written job description. Selection criteria should be imbedded in the job description.

5. Consider various incentives that will attract the highest caliber peer leader possible.

6. Create a peer leader application packet that includes the necessary information to allow potential peer leaders to submit quality applications, which provide the selection committee with information upon which to base sound decisions.

7. Consider multiple and creative avenues for the recruitment of potential peer leaders.

8. Use the peer leader recruitment phase to create a public relations campaign for the program.

9. Involve a wide variety of individuals in the selection process to increase the likelihood of good and equitable decisions.

10. Take adequate time to conduct a thorough selection process, considering a variety of selection tools (i.e., application, nominations, interviews, etc.).

11. Develop and implement a training program that is comprehensive in approach and that provides peer leaders with the information, skills, and inspiration they will need to be effective in their roles.

12. Assess and evaluate all aspects of the peer leader program frequently for use in future development and program refinements.

References

Astin, A. (1984). Student involvement: A developmental theory for higher education. *Journal of College Student Personnel, 25,* 297-308.

Brown, S., & Cook, T. (1999). The winning team: A training model for faculty/staff and peer educators. *Proceedings of the twelfth international conference of the first-year experience* (pp. 117-118). Columbia, SC: University of South Carolina, National Resource Center for The First-Year Experience and Students in Transition.

Carroll, L. (1990). *More annotated Alice: Alice's adventures in wonderland and through the looking-glass and what Alice found there.* New York: Random House.

Casady, M. J. (1999). Building the peer leader and teacher team. *Proceedings of the eighteenth annual conference of the first-year experience* (pp. 180-181). Columbia, SC: University of South Carolina, National Resource Center for The First-Year Experience and Students in Transition.

Chickering, A. W. (1969). *Education and identity*. San Francisco: Jossey-Bass.

Chickering, A. W., & Reisser, L. (1993). *Education and identity* (2nd Ed.). San Francisco: Jossey-Bass.

Ender, S. C., & Newton, F. B. (2000). *Students helping students: A guide for peer educators on college campuses*. San Francisco: Jossey-Bass.

Gardner, J. N. (1981). Developing faculty as facilitators and mentors. In V. A. Harren (Ed.), Facilitating student's career development (pp. 67-79). *New Directions for Student Services, 14.* San Francisco: Jossey-Bass.

Goldsweig, S. (1999). Leadership in action: A class for training peer mentors in the art of leadership. *Proceedings of the eighteenth annual conference of the first-year experience* (p. 29). Columbia, SC: University of South Carolina, National Resource Center for The First-Year Experience and Students in Transition.

Hamid, S. L., & VanHook, J. (1999). [Peer Leader Program Questionnaire]. Unpublished raw data. (Available from the Office of First-Year Programs, Lee University, Cleveland, TN, 37320-3450).

Hunter, S. M, & Cuseo, J. B. (1999). Ensuring the success of faculty training workshops. In M. S. Hunter, & T. L. Skipper (Eds.), *Solid foundations: Building success for first-year seminars through instructor training and development* (Monograph No. 29) (pp. 73-83). Columbia, SC: University of South Carolina, National Resource Center for The First-Year Experience and Students in Transition.

Lybrand, D., & Kieffer, T. (1999). How an innovative team teaching approach works at one private liberal arts institution. *Proceedings of the 1999 national conference on students in transition-west* (p. 91). Columbia, SC: University of South Carolina, National Resource Center for The First-Year Experience and Students in Transition.

National Resource Center for The First-Year Experience & Students in Transition. (1997). National survey of first-year seminar programs. Unpublished instrument. (Available from Author, University of South Carolina, Columbia SC, 29208).

Orazem, V., Buchanan, T., & Roller, A. (1998). A successful peer leader program: A conversation with student coordinators. *Proceedings of the seventeenth annual conference of the first-year experience* (p. 115). Columbia, SC: University of South Carolina, National Resource Center for The First-Year Experience and Students in Transition.

Perry, W. G., Jr. (1968). *Forms of intellectual and ethical development in the college years: A scheme.* New York: Holt, Rinehart, & Winston.

Priser, T. L., Johnson, J., & McCarthy, K. (1999). Peers training peers: Utilizing returning peer leaders in the training process. *Proceedings of the eighteenth annual conference of the first-year experience* (p. 73). Columbia, SC: University of South Carolina, National Resource Center for The First-Year Experience and Students in Transition.

Staley, C. (1999). Facilitating a group. In M. S. Hunter, & T. L. Skipper (Eds.), *Solid foundations: Building success for first-year seminars through instructor training and development* (Monograph No. 29) (pp. 67-72). Columbia, SC: University of South Carolina, National Resource Center for The First-Year Experience and Students in Transition.

Whitman, N. A. (1988). *Peer teaching: To teach is to learn twice.* (ASHE-ERIC Higher Education Report No. 4) Washington, DC: Association for the Study of Higher Education.

CHAPTER 5

CREATIVE PEER LEADERSHIP: BEYOND THE CLASSROOM

Marmy Clason and John Beck*

W ithin any institution, upperclass students clearly impact the academic success and
social well-being of first-year students. This mentoring has often been serendipi-
tous, leading to both favorable and unfavorable outcomes. But one thing is certain; this mentoring has proven to be powerful and efficient. Therefore, institutions
are seeking to harness this powerful, peer force in order to shape their campus community.
This chapter will catalogue the thoughtful, creative, and strategic use of peer leaders outside
the first-year seminar classroom. A review of the literature in this area suggests that past
research in this area has not done justice to the exciting and creative ways in which peers are
impacting first-year students. For this chapter, therefore, we investigated the use of peers
within existing programs at colleges and universities across the United States.

In our review of peer leadership, we discovered programs that address the academic and
social needs of matriculating students. Peer leaders are enhancing the academic experience of
first-year students by serving as academic peer advisors, Supplemental Instruction leaders,
and mentors for probationary students. We also found that peers enhance social experience
by serving as orientation leaders, residence hall leaders, cohort group leaders, and as liaisons
who address health issues and the needs of underrepresented populations. This chapter will
offer examples of programs currently functioning in each of these areas.

Academic Needs

Academic Advising

As first-year students matriculate, they face a variety of challenges. Foremost among them is
the need to understand the components of their academic program and the need to orchestrate
a successful course of study (Gordon, 1992). Since it is essential for first-year students to engage in this process early, a staff or faculty member has traditionally been assigned as the

*The authors wish to thank Patricia Ramone and Louis Vangieri of Delaware Technical and Community College,
Wilmington Campus for their insightful contributions to this chapter on the use of peer leaders on community college
campuses. Their investigation illuminates the variety of ways peers can be used to influence first-year students.

academic advisor. But today, students are sometimes meeting the need by serving as peer academic advisors. By serving as a link between first-year students and the institution's academic advising system, trained peer advisors do not replace faculty, but rather complement them.

This type of peer advising may occur in connection with the first-year seminar class. For example, at Austin College (Sherman, Texas), one of the peer advisors' responsibilities is to "provide informed academic advising" on a one-to-one basis throughout the semester. In contrast, the University of North Texas (UNT) in Denton has created a program that specifically uses undergraduates as academic advisors. They are recruited from all UNT colleges and academic areas. These academic peer advisors participate in one week of training at the beginning of the semester, supplemented by two-hour weekly staff meetings during the semester. Peer advisors, like faculty or staff advisors, must keep office hours. However, they keep office hours in an academic resource office created within a residence hall. The peer advisors live in the hall just like the residence assistants and are compensated with a private room and a stipend. UNT believes this type of interaction enhances the academic advising system by increasing advising availability and by offering the unique, student perspective on the advising process. The opportunity to meet with a peer in the residence hall not only makes advising more convenient, it also diminishes the anxiety first-year students may feel in approaching a faculty or staff advisor.

Supplemental Instruction

Effective advising will bring first-year students into the right classroom, but their success in that classroom depends on their ability to grasp the content and employ effective study techniques. While some study strategies learned at the secondary level will adapt to the college or university setting, successful students will modify their approach when faced

with the more demanding challenges of the classroom after high school (Walter, Gomon, Guenzel, & Smith, 1989). This modification is enhanced by the use of peer leaders in programs like Supplemental Instruction (Arendale, 1994). Developed at the University of Missouri-Kansas City, Supplemental Instruction (SI) uses peer leaders to lead study sessions in traditionally difficult classes. The goals of SI are to improve student performance, to foster retention, and to improve learning skills. The program targets classes that produce a large number of D-F grades and are subject to high student-withdrawal rates. The program supervisor works with faculty who teach these courses to select students who have achieved a high course grade, have good interpersonal skills, and are well-organized. These students, called SI leaders, facilitate volunteer study sessions, which occur outside the regular class time. These one-hour study sessions meet three to five times a week. During these sessions, the SI leader helps the participants understand the course material and enhances specific study strategies aimed at mastering the course content. The sessions are highly interactive with the SI leaders serving as facilitators for large and small group discussion. SI leaders are generally compensated with an hourly wage or stipend. This intervention is designed to intercept and overcome the academic challenges first-year students may face in traditionally difficult classes and has been adopted by colleges and universities throughout the country.

Supplemental Instruction is also employed by community colleges. The program at Orchard Ridge Campus of Oakland Community College in Farmington Hills, Michigan involves peer group leaders who provide SI in more than 100 courses at a variety of levels from developmental to advanced. The college indicates that this assistance has had a positive effect on students' study skill development and expected academic achievement. Delta College in University Center, Michigan, offers a similar Peer Mentor and Structured Learning

Assistance Program. The program uses the SI model to encourage students to take responsibility for their own learning.

Academically At-Risk Students

Some students will need help beyond the traditionally difficult courses. These students may be underprepared for college work or may be uninformed about many aspects of the culture of higher education. How can peer leaders impact these students who need additional support and guidance? Concordia University Wisconsin (Mequon, Wisconsin) has piloted a one-credit class for at-risk students. The seminar, entitled "Learning Strategies," is required of students whose failure in the academic arena has resulted in academic probation and is limited to 15 participants. The course is designed to assist students in overcoming the obstacles blocking their path to academic success. Here, students engage in self-discovery exercises in order to identify obstacles to their growth and to implement strategies for overcoming those obstacles. A variety of challenges are addressed including study skills, career indecision, and the social forces of student life. Former probationary students who have overcome those challenges offer valuable insights to the student on probation. They are invited into a class session to lead informal discussions on a single topic identified as a need by the class. The peer leader reinforces positive attitudes, affirms positive behaviors, and offers the hope of future success. These peer leaders receive no training or compensation but are eager to share their insights as they celebrate their success.

Social Needs

The success or failure of first-year students is not merely a matter of academics. The social forces that surround them during their first year pull matriculating students in a number of different directions. Peer leaders clearly influence the academic success of first-year students by helping them negotiate these competing demands. But equally, if not more important, is the strategic use of peers to impact the social well-being of these students. At colleges and universities around the United States, peers are at work as orientation leaders, residence hall leaders, cohort group leaders, and as liaisons who address health issues and underrepresented populations.

Orientation

The initial contact first-year students have with peer leaders is often with upperclass students involved in orientation. Traditionally, pre-semester orientation to the campus has been the responsibility of student-service personnel. But continuing students have become more and more integral to the process. Generally, such orientation programs are designed to support and celebrate the arrival of new students. This includes orienting new students to key academic issues, social issues, the campus environment, and college services.

> Supplemental Instruction (SI) uses peers to lead study sessions in traditionally difficult classes. The goals of SI are to improve student performance, to foster retention, and to improve

The program at Marquette University (Milwaukee, Wisconsin) is paradigmatic of universities using student orientation leaders to accomplish these goals. Each orientation leader is assigned a group of approximately 20 new students with whom they will work over the orientation week. These small groups remain together in order to foster the development of meaningful friendships, to become acquainted with the campus, and to discuss important social issues. One of the highlights of these five days is the dramatic performance written and presented by orientation leaders. New students are confronted with scenarios they might face on this urban campus like substance abuse, date rape, eating disorders, and encounters with the homeless. Peer leaders facilitate breakout groups to discuss the topics following the presentation. Five full-time student leaders oversee and administer the program. The university reimburses these five student leaders. They train the 120 volunteer, orientation leaders over three days addressing both the content of this initial orientation and the process through which the content is shared.

> These meetings take place in locations where students and faculty usually do not interact, and their primary goal is to build relationships between members of the cohort group and the teaching team

While the orientation program at Marquette University concentrates its intervention during the first week of school, Indiana University Southeast (New Albany, Indiana) has a different approach. The Student Ambassador Program at IU Southeast interacts with students over a longer period of time. This program uses juniors and seniors as liaisons between the university and community at large and as leaders in the orientation process. The goals of this program are to provide a smooth transition for new IU Southeast students and to create a comfortable atmosphere for those new students. During summer orientation sessions, the Ambassadors share personal experiences from their own educational life at IU Southeast and offer suggestions for making a successful transition to the campus. After the summer orientation session, these peers make six additional contacts with the incoming IU Southeast students. Four of these contacts occur prior to the fall semester. They consist of two postcards, one newsletter, and one telephone contact. Ambassadors also maintain contact throughout the first year, with a minimum of two contacts within the first six weeks of school. The Ambassadors use these con-

tacts to convey a warm welcome to these new arrivals. Each Ambassador works with approximately 28 students. The Ambassadors have a rigorous training schedule that finds the students meeting weekly throughout the spring semester. This is followed by a one-day retreat in the summer. The Ambassadors receive training in areas such as working with students with disabilities, sexual assault and harassment, interpersonal conflict, personality assessment, and university policy. The Ambassadors are awarded two academic credits for their participation in this program and given a letter grade.

This extended mentoring approach is also used at the community college level. Skagit Valley College in Mount Vernon, Washington offers a collaborative mentoring program in paralegal, office and business, and business management training programs. The goal of the program is to connect first-year students to peer mentors. Peer Guides, as these students are called, provide campus tours and information tables at the beginning of each new term. They offer new student support and follow up during the first two weeks of each term in order to develop mentoring relationships. The Peer Guide training program includes communication skills and group leadership skills. The leaders of the Peer Guide program have also created a handbook for faculty and student mentors.

Similarly, the College of Southern Idaho in Twin Falls offers a one-on-one peer mentoring program. The student mentors, called Friends on Campus, help staff members conduct workshops, visit classrooms, and organize classroom activities. Each is assigned no more than two incoming students, many of whom are nontraditional in age. The Friends on Campus themselves are supported during monthly meetings throughout the semester. At these meetings, they discuss issues related to their participation in the program or their student life in general. The college has identified peer mentoring as one of the most important factors in helping reentry students feel comfortable in the educational setting.

First-Year Programs in the Residence Halls

Although it is essential that first-year students are oriented to the campus environment prior to the start of the semester, the most effective orientation continues throughout the semester, particularly in the residence halls (Perigo & Upcraft, 1989; Upcraft, 1989a). Together with resident hall directors and resident hall assistants, peer leaders play a role in helping students maintain their sense of well-being throughout the first year. The University of Guelph's (Guelph, Ontario) program called University College Connection (UCC) is one such program using undergraduates as resident hall leaders. Students who choose to participate in the UCC program are grouped into "clusters" of 15 to 30 students who are pursuing the same degree program. A student who is called a "cluster leader" facilitates each cluster. On campus, cluster participants live in a common area with the cluster leader.

The goals of this program are to build community, promote collaborative learning, promote faculty and student interaction, share effective learning strategies, and promote the independence and resourcefulness of cluster participants. In order to accomplish those goals, cluster groups meet weekly for the first six weeks of the semester. In these formal meetings, the peers lead sessions that include interaction with faculty and other guest speakers. The cluster leader also interacts informally with their cluster members on a daily basis. Occasionally, several cluster groups will join together at events coordinated by the cluster group leaders.

During a four-day workshop, peer leaders receive training in the particulars of the program. This includes an introduction to group building, issues faced by first-year students, and university resources designed to support student success.

At Trinity College (Hartford, Connecticut) all the first-year residents live in one of six first-year residence halls. These halls are designed to create a "vibrant academic and social community," where upperclass students act as "mentors." These peer mentors live in the hall with first-year students and participate in a first-year seminar class composed of residents from that hall. This again allows for both formal and informal interaction between the peer mentor and students on topics like decision-making, campus resources, multiculturalism, and study skills. The training of the peer mentors parallels the training done by Guelph but is done over one week and is supported by workshops during the semester and monthly meetings. Both institutions compensate these students for their contribution with a stipend.

Although these peer cluster leaders and mentors interact in the formal classroom environment, perhaps the greatest benefit is the informal interaction produced from the living arrangements in the residence halls (Upcraft, 1989a). To quote the project director at the University at Albany (SUNY), "This contact puts them [residence hall leaders] in a better position to know the needs of students in general and to recognize when a particular student is struggling" (P. Sawyer, personal communication, October 6, 1999).

Cohort Groups

The social needs of first-year students are also met through a variety of peer-lead mechanisms summarized under the heading of cohort groups. At Concordia University Wisconsin in Mequon, the cohort group is associated with the first-year seminar class. The 20-member class is divided into four cohort groups. The teaching team, composed of the instructor and peer leader, schedules an out-of-class meeting with the cohort group led by the peer leader. These meetings take place in locations where students and faculty usually do not interact, and their primary goal is to build relationships between members of the cohort group and the teaching team. These enhanced relationships not only benefit the individual student in their socialization process but also enhance the spirit of community in the seminar classroom (Beck & Clason, 1999).

This small-group interaction takes place once every two weeks throughout the semester. The cohort group itself is responsible for selecting the location of the meeting, and each member receives points for attendance toward the final grade. These meetings take place in residence hall rooms, campus lounges, and local restaurants. Each meeting lasts at least 30 minutes during which the peer leader invites the students to talk about their transition experiences. More often than not, these conversations focus on social matters like roommate problems, dating relationships, and homesickness. Students react positively to these meetings and speak highly of their value. As one student put it:

> I feel that I have made some great friendships through this group. At first, I only knew one other person in my group. But now I know all of them quite well. I hope to keep these friendships throughout the rest of college. These are some great friends and I know I can trust them and talk to them about anything.

There is no doubt that the success of these meetings hinges upon the leadership and accessibility created by the peer leader (Beck & Clason, 1999).

Cohort groups are also employed on other campuses independent of the first-year seminar course. In the College of Fine Arts at the University of Nebraska at Omaha, continuing students are used to mentor cohort groups. The goals of this cohort program are to enhance the students' study skills, to aid students in establishing appropriate goals, and to understand what it means to be a student of the arts. Each cohort group consists of 10 to 15 students from the same department and is led

by a peer mentor who is also from that department. The mentors meet with their cohort group once every week, but no academic credit is earned by the students participating. The peer mentors invite their cohorts to participate in group-building activities, journaling, and other classroom exercises. These exercises enhance the students' time management skills and goal-setting skills. The mentors also inform the students about campus services and invite them to view their success in a holistic way. The Retention Project Coordinator trains these students for their role by involving them in all the activities and content they will present. The peer mentors also find themselves to be a "cohort group" since they meet with the program's coordinator once a week. The mentors receive an hourly wage from the university for their service.

Guilford College (Greensboro, North Carolina) also makes use of a cohort group unassociated with a first-year success course. The peer mentor is paired with a group of four to six matriculating students with whom the peer meets weekly for the first half of the semester. The mentor's interaction with the students is directed by a resource guide that includes a weekly topic (e.g., learning styles, diversity, study skills), group activities, and homework assignments. During the second half of the semester, the peer mentor meets individually with each student in the group. In the one-on-one meetings, the peer mentor continues to assess how the student is progressing and makes suggestions for the remainder of the semester.

Health and Wellness

Yet another way in which peer leaders are improving the lives of first-year students is in connection with institution-sponsored health initiatives. Western Kentucky University (Bowling Green, Kentucky) has such a program called Peers Encouraging Responsible Choices (PERC). The goals of this program are to promote healthy lifestyles and responsible decision making, specifically in the areas of alcohol and other drug use, self-esteem, and sexual behavior. Because research indicates that college students overestimate the number of their peers who drink heavily and participate in other risky behaviors (Berkowitz, 1987, 1998), PERC peer leaders work to set the record straight and encourage responsible choices in social situations. Peer educators work closely with the health education staff, but these peer educators decide which issues are addressed and what educational activities they provide on campus. PERC is associated with the BACCHUS and GAMMA Peer Education Network. Any Western Kentucky University student is eligible for membership in this student-run organization. The peer educators are trained in conjunction with the program materials provided through this national organization.

First-year seminar instructors invite one or two of these PERC peer educators to present their program within the seminar classroom. They seek to provide first-year students with an accurate view of alcohol use at Western Kentucky University, to challenge their attitudes about getting drunk, to speak about the effects of alcohol on the body, and to address the subject of alcohol poisoning. These peers also interact with the campus community apart from the first-year seminar class. Just prior to spring break, PERC leaders set up an information table to encourage attitudes and behaviors that would result in a fun but safe vacation. They sponsor awareness campaigns such as Healthy Loving (sexual responsibility week), Eating Disorder Awareness Week, World AIDS Day, and The Great American Smokeout. They also organize events for the campus at large. For example, many college students believe that a fun Thursday night has to involve the use of alcohol and other drugs and other forms of unhealthy behavior. PERC schedules a Thursday night alcohol-free party called Midnight Volleyball, where students enjoy free food, mocktails, live music, and a volleyball tournament.

The PERC program at Western Kentucky University demonstrates how powerful peer leaders can be when addressing the physical and relational well-being of first-year students. Program leaders have seen that adult members of the campus community have not always found their insights and suggestions on these topics warmly received by a student audience. PERC leaders believe undergraduates are not only more successful at initiating this type of conversation but also that they are more likely to affect changes in behavior and attitudes of first-year students.

Underrepresented Populations

Peer leaders also are addressing the unique needs of traditionally underrepresented populations on college and university campuses. These students may face challenges that exceed the challenges faced by majority students (Upcraft, 1989b). This has led many colleges and universities to design interventions that support the success of these underrepresented students. The Welcome Program at the University of Texas-Austin provides support as well as a networking opportunity for underrepresented students. This intervention takes two forms, a mentor program and a cohort program. The goals of the mentor program are to develop the skills necessary for students to succeed in college, to motivate students toward academic excellence, to create success through caring, and to provide a resource person. The program matches first-year students with upperclass students who have shown an interest in providing support for new students. These peers meet with their mentees once a week to speak about concerns they may have and to discuss matters related to success. For example, the mentor may discuss major and career goals, introduce the student to others on campus, encourage involvement in campus activities, visit the gym with his or her mentee for a joint workout, introduce campus services like the computer lab, and help the student organize his or her time.

The second arm of the Welcome Program involves cohort groups. The goal of the cohort program is to provide students a foundation upon which to build relationships so that they may make a smooth transition into campus life. Students choose which cohort they would like to join. Some of the cohort groups are based on race and ethnicity, while others are based on undergraduate college or hometown. The cohort groups are composed of 10 first-year students and one upperclass peer leader. The responsibility of the peer leader is to plan monthly cohort group meetings, to motivate members of the group in their pursuit of academic success, and to serve as a resource and referral person for the group. These meetings address content similar to the individual mentor meetings. Mentors and cohort group leaders are trained in a one-day workshop where they receive an information packet and engage with speakers who address leadership, motivation, and diversity. These mentors receive no compensation or credit, but enjoy special social activities and award ceremonies.

The State University of West Georgia (Carrollton, Georgia) also has a peer leader program designed to impact the success of underrepresented populations. The Minority Achievement Program (MAP) uses upperclass peer mentors in order to increase the retention of minority students, to increase their academic performance, and to expedite their social integration to campus. Matriculating students are encouraged to sign up for a peer mentor during the summer or fall orientation program. However, they may enroll in the program at any time during the first year. Peer mentors are each assigned a group of 10 to 12 first-year, minority students whom they contact both by mail and phone. Throughout the year, mentors hold office hours during which they meet individually with their assigned students. The mentors offer academic tutoring and discuss campus services and adjustment issues. The peer leaders also work together to create programming that addresses the special needs of the minority students on cam-

pus. The MAP peer mentors are given one day of training during which they receive a manual that summarizes the program and the responsibilities of the mentor. They also engage in sessions on effective listening and learning techniques. A small stipend is offered for their service.

At Metropolitan Community College in Omaha, Nebraska, an Ambassador Program offers a variety of peer activities at the college with a focus on outreach to new students. The underlying purpose of the program is to enhance the international and intercultural environment of the institution by providing support for non-English and English speaking students. Ambassadors offer presentations to the larger college community on diverse cultural themes and on how to live harmoniously together. Each ambassador is trained in communication, listening, and presentation skills and cultural awareness and is given information on all campus services.

Peer leaders are also used to help disseminate cross-cultural programming at the community-college level. At Delaware Technical & Community College Stanton/Wilmington Campus, the Peer Associate program involves exemplary second-year students who complete a rigorous application process. Peer Associates, who receive a bookstore scholarship for their participation, are involved in a variety of student service-related activities, including work with cross-cultural programming throughout the campus. The cross-cultural seminars are created to promote an understanding of student commonalties and to honor student differences. Because of the great diversity on campus, more than 50 countries are represented in these seminars. To ensure a quality program, Peer Associates are provided information on multi-culturalism, taught effective presentation skills, and coached as cross-cultural group facilitators. Peer Associates lead eight seminars over an academic year. The seminars bring together first-year students enrolled in the "Mastering

College Life" course with English as a Second Language (ESL) students enrolled in "Advanced Listening and Speaking." The content of the seminars includes understanding human diversity, building cross-cultural leadership skills, critical thinking for a diverse world, and working effectively in cross-cultural teams. Each seminar follows a standard agenda, which includes the following activities:

≪ Introduction—A micro lecture sets up the topic and explains the small group work to follow.
≪ Collaborative Activity—Students work in small cross-cultural groups on an active learning exercise.
≪ Large Group Processing—Students are brought back together to summarize their findings.
≪ Journaling—Students share their cross-cultural experience through free writing.

Peer Associates on the Wilmington Campus also participate in the institution's first-year success course. Some training for peer leaders is provided through a specially created one-credit academic course entitled "Becoming a Peer Helper," designed to build peer helping and leadership skills.

This overview demonstrates that peer leaders are at work beyond the first-year seminar classroom. Peer leader programs have found a home in all parts of the country and within a wide range of public and private colleges and universities. The prominence of these programs in American higher education signals a clear belief that peer leaders impact the academic and social well-being of their fellow students. It is also clear that peer leadership programs assume a variety of forms from orientation to academic support. The programs impact students of various backgrounds and in many stages of development, suggesting that peer leaders have the ability to influence students in a wide variety of settings and circumstances. Despite this variety, these programs share similar goals. They seek to wel-

come new students, acclimate them to the institution's life, and retain them by giving them the support needed to succeed academically and socially.

Because peer leaders add insight and credibility to the college or university's efforts to assimilate new students, these programs tap into the powerful influence that upperclass students wield in the lives of younger students. In recognition of this fact, many institutions are seeking to harness this powerful resource in order to shape a positive experience for their first-year students.

References

Arendale, D. R. (1994). Understanding the supplemental instruction model. *New Directions for Teaching and Learning, 60,* 11-21.

Beck, J. A., & Clason, M. A. (1999, February). *The cohort group model: A new approach to building relationships in your FYE class.* Paper presented at the 19th Annual Conference on The First-Year Experience and Students in Transition, Columbia, SC.

Berkowitz, A. D. (1987). Current issues in effective alcohol education programming. In J. S. Sherwood (Ed.), *Alcohol policies and practices on college and university campuses* (pp. 69-85). Washington, DC: National Association of Student Personnel Administrators.

Berkowitz, A. D. (1998, October). *Turning peer culture on itself: Helping students translate healthy beliefs into healthy actions.* Paper presented at a one-day workshop on alcohol issues facing college campuses at Edgewood College, Madison, WI.

Gordon, V. (1992). *Handbook of academic advising.* New York: Greenwood Press.

Perigo, D. J., & Upcraft, M. L. (1989). Orientation programs. Academic support programs. In M. L. Upcraft & J. N. Gardner (Eds.), *The freshman year experience* (pp. 82-94). San Francisco: Jossey-Bass.

Upcraft, M. L. (1989a). Residence halls and campus activities. Academic support programs. In M. L. Upcraft & J. N. Gardner (Eds.),

The freshman year experience (pp. 142-155). San Francisco: Jossey-Bass.

Upcraft, M. L. (1989b). Understanding student development: Insights from theory. In M. L. Upcraft & J. N. Gardner (Eds.), *The freshman year experience* (pp. 40-52). San Francisco: Jossey-Bass.

Walter, T. L., Gomon, A., Guenzel, P. J., & Smith, D. E. P. (1989). Academic support programs. In M. L. Upcraft & J. N. Gardner (Eds.), *The freshman year experience* (pp. 108-117). San Francisco: Jossey-Bass.

CHAPTER 6

PEER LEADERSHIP AND INSTRUCTIONAL TECHNOLOGIES

Jean M. Henscheid and Gary Brown

Reuben has never met Pedro and Marisa has never seen Brenda, but these four students have, nevertheless, changed each other's lives. Pedro and Brenda are troubled youths who have lived in, and left, a string of foster homes. Reuben and Marisa are Hypernauts, undergraduate peer leaders who work with students over the Internet. With the Hypernauts' help, Pedro and Brenda and other at-risk students have learned to interact in World Wide Web-based threaded discussions and chat rooms, to research careers on the Internet, to write lucid and thoughtful comments to their distant peers, and to build a new kind of community with other students who have shared similarly difficult experiences. E-mail, according to one of the youths, "has changed my life."

The work that Marisa and Reuben do as online peer leaders, while special, is not unique. Across and beyond the United States, a new brand of peer leaders is accomplishing with ease what their elders in colleges and universities are managing with some trepidation—integrating learning, instruction, and new technologies. From installing software and hauling hardware, to making purchasing decisions and providing online instruction, peer leaders are working with, and in some instances leading, their institutions in the great race to enter the knowledge age.

In this chapter, we will outline a rationale for integrating peer leadership and instructional technologies, beginning with a general discussion of the issues surrounding their burgeoning use. Then, drawing on examples from throughout the United States, we will make the argument that the marriage of instructional technologies and peer leadership offers traditional institutions a chance to survive another, related, contest—the race to attract students that sees new competitors, for-profit, employer-sponsored, and strictly online institutions, entering at a rapid rate.

From Unique to Ubiquitous

While a pencil, construction paper, or a glue stick, in the hands of teachers and students, can all be considered instructional technologies, for purposes of this chapter, the definitions offered by Tucker (1995) will help draw stricter parameters around our meaning of the phrase. This spectrum of new learning environments available on campuses today, according to Tucker, include one-way audio/visual classrooms, two-way audio/visual classrooms, two-way audio classrooms, two-way audio graphic classrooms, desktop groupware conferencing, desktop video conferencing, asynchronous desktop conferencing, and asynchronous/CD-ROM hybrids (which permit fax storage and retrieval and voice mail services). As is discussed below, peer leaders are involved in helping students, and faculty members, in both campus-based and distance courses, in real-time and asynchronously, as they use many of these new technologies.

There is general agreement that at this, the dawning of a new millennium, these technologies are having impacts equivalent to those of the Industrial Revolution of the late eighteenth and early nineteenth centuries (Drucker, 1999). Within and outside higher education, these and other new technologies are widely available. Jupiter Research predicts that by 2001, the Internet will be in more than 50 million households in the United States and, by 2002, the population seeking their information online will rival that of the number of consumers of cable television and newspapers. Between 75% and 80% of households with children and incomes of $40,000 or more are now equipped with personal computers. Almost half of U.S. citizens between the ages of 16 and 22 (comprising a tenth of the overall population) are online and 84% of American college students surf the Internet from their residence hall room or another campus location (Schiewe, 1999). As new industries emerge employing new knowledge workers and as existing processes are transformed in nearly every sector of the economy, colleges and universities are faced with keeping up with these changes and with preparing citizens, and workers, for this new age. First, the educational attempt to respond has resulted in a surge of effort to wire campus buildings appropriately. In 1994, only 3% of all classrooms in the U.S. had Internet access. By 1998, that number had jumped to 51%. At the same time, however, the Department of Education reported that 80% of teachers felt unprepared to integrate computers into their classroom instruction (Schiewe, 1999).

Ready or not, computing and information technology are becoming core components of both the classroom experience and the campus environment. A 1998 survey on campus computing indicated that 44.4% of classes use e-mail, 33% use Internet resources, 45.1% of undergraduates and 51.6% of faculty use the Internet at least once a day, and 45.8% of campuses have instituted mandatory student technology fees. The numbers climb every year (Green, 1999).

How Best To Make It Work?

Because the costs associated with retooling and rewiring campuses are high (Twigg, 1997), it follows that educators are seeking answers to the question, "how do we make it work for students?" Many are asking, what is the impact on learning of the use of e-mail as the primary communications medium between faculty and students? How do threaded discussions impact the interactions among students and the academic products they produce? How has multimedia, researching on the Internet, and creating World Wide Web pages enhanced the students' ability to think critically or solve complex problems? Consistent with the educational research "answers" that came before, those related to information technology are just as complex. For every study revealing that the introduction of instructional technologies is "good," it seems there is one to suggest that it is "bad." In the negative corner, Russell's (1996) findings suggest the reluctance to change when he reports that even though students perceive that technology will make learning easier, more enjoyable, more accessible, and more flexible, they would still elect a traditional classroom. Weighing in for technology advocates, Kern (1995) found that students in two beginning college courses had more opportunities to speak and used a greater variety of discourse functions when working with a particular software program than they did in oral discussions. There is little doubt that "how do we make it work?" and related questions, as Kern's findings presage, will be redefined because information technology is a moving target. We are already seeing how the meanings of the question, "does it work?" are changed by our efforts to integrate and assess the impacts of those technologies on learning. Moreover, the technologies themselves are changing, and what we want our students to do with technologies changes as well. Further, as students begin to use a greater variety of discourse functions associated with different software programs, those different discourse functions will increasingly lend themselves to greater scrutiny. Similar questions, in fact, have been explored ever since visual instructional materials were ushered into the classrooms of 1928 (Saettler, 1968).

What seems the clearest caution for educator and researcher is that "if teachers merely add technology on to ineffective instructional methods, if we electrify our lecture halls, there will be no improvement in student learning" (Twigg, 1997, p. 3). This recognition has prompted some instructors to turn their attention to the "how do we make it work" question in more traditional venues, to ask questions related to the effectiveness of teaching strategies in general. Along the way, some have rediscovered collaborative and cooperative learning approaches (Bruffee 1995; Twigg 1997; Johnson, Johnson, & Smith, 1998), a pedagogy with direct application to the use of peer leaders. The fit between instructional technology and group learning pedagogy, according to Johnson (1996) and Twigg (1997), is a good one, with educators finding that new technologies enable "changes in pedagogy, a paradigm shift to more individualized, self-paced mastery learning" and education that takes advantage of activity-based learning, cooperation between students, and hands-on experiences (Twigg, 1997, p. 3). The notion that students should interact with other students in the classroom, in whatever form it takes,

has, according to Johnson, Johnson, and Smith (1998), returned to college.

Cooperation and Collaboration Revisited

These cooperative and collaborative pedagogies capitalize on a force recognized as singularly powerful in undergraduate education—the capacity of students to influence their peers. In matters ranging from academic major and course selection to political and ethical choices, this effect is solidly documented (for example, see Astin, 1977; Dalton, 1985; Dey, 1989; Komarovsky, 1985; Lane, 1968; Mallinckrodt, 1988; Moffatt, 1989; Newcomb & Wilson, 1966; Pascarella, 1980; Pascarella & Terenzini, 1980; Pascarella & Terenzini, 1981; and Vreeland & Bidwell, 1965). These influences have been noted in and outside the classroom. A study of 2,050 second-year college students revealed that collaborative learning (when students in groups organize their own learning situations and set their own goals) leads to gains in cognitive and affective levels and openness to diversity (Cabrera, Nora, Bernal, Terenzini, & Pascarella, 1998). Collaborative learning practices, the authors suggest, can maximize learning and create a positive, productive environment for challenging students' preconceptions. Ohta (1995) noted similar gains when students collaborated to learn Japanese as a second language. Results of another study reported by Wathen and Resnick (1997) suggest that peer-to-peer collaboration creates an environment conducive to the generation of explanations from one student to another. Generation of these explanations,

> "if teachers merely add technology on to ineffective instructional methods, if we electrify our lecture halls, there will be no improvement in student learning" (Twigg, 1997, p. 3).

defined by the authors as new inferences that went beyond the text material, was highly predictive of both factual and conceptual learning.

Results of research on cooperative learning, when students work together to achieve pre-set learning outcomes, "leave little doubt that cooperative learning is appropriate to higher education; it works" (Johnson, et al., 1998, pp. 27-28). A meta-analysis of 305 studies conducted between 1924 and 1997 comparing the relative efficiency and effectiveness of cooperative, competitive, and individualist learning revealed that cooperative learning promotes higher academic achievement than other modes; encourages increased liking among students; increases a perception of support among students; promotes higher self-esteem; improves students' attitudes toward learning; and has the greatest impact on students' willingness to develop and change their values, attitudes, and behavioral patterns. Finally, cooperative learning promotes heightened meta-cognitive thought, creativity in problem solving, higher reasoning abilities, intrinsic motivation, transfer of learning from one situation to another, greater time on task, and a greater willingness to accept difficult tasks (Johnson, et al., 1998).

Specifically related to cooperative and collaborative learning as well as the learning of computer skills, working with peers has been correlated with reduced anxiety and increased motivation by enhancing the students' sense of control and competence (McInerney, 1996). To conduct the study, McInerney placed high and low anxious students in both direct instruction and cooperative, self-regulated learning groups, with the latter offering the greatest gains in increased motivation and decreased anxiety. Extending and sharpening the implications of collaborative approaches to learning, designated peer tutors can perhaps enhance collaborative and cooperative learning approaches even more. An earlier discourse analysis conducted by Merrill, Reiser,

Merrill, and Landes (1995) revealed that in tutor-student sessions in which the students were learning computer programming language, successful tutors took "an active role in leading the problem-solving process by offering confirmatory feedback and additional guidance while students are on profitable paths and error feedback after mistakes" (p. 315). In 1992, Merrill, Reiser, Ranney, and Trafton suggested that successful peer tutors offer rapid and explicit feedback to student actions, informing students whether their actions were correct or not. When mistakes were made, the researchers found that students and tutors work together to repair the errors and that tutors provide feedback measured to allow students to perform many aspects of the error recovery process.

Combining Instructional Technologies and Peer Leadership—Current Practices

Recognizing these benefits, instructors are yoking the introduction of new technologies in their classrooms to assignments and activities that offer students, from kindergarten to college, opportunities to collaborate and cooperate. In many instances, the instructors are sharing leadership in the classroom with students who offer a variety of services to both other students and their instructors. Many undergraduates are literally growing up with this form of peer support. In elementary schools, students have been engaged as technical mentors, tutors, helpers, and experts. In one fifth grade class, students were assigned as computer tutors to other students, while in a sixth grade classroom at another school, female students were used as experts in a workshop introducing a computer-based learning environment to other students (Hodges, 1997). The results of the later experience were that students successfully completed their tasks, they relied upon the female peer experts, and those experts benefited from the experience (Edwards, Coddington, & Caterina, 1997). In some elementary and middle schools, "tech teams" have been formed and a step-by-step manual has been produced to aid in replication of the practice elsewhere (Peto, Onishi, & Irish, 1998). At the high school level, students in the Monett Schools in Missouri are stationed in "control rooms" to assist their peers and teachers throughout the district in uses of technology. Benefits of this approach, according to program administrators, include increased teacher self-reliance and increased self-esteem among students providing the service (Ingram, 1998). In another high school, senior-level peer tutors assisted other students in the use of an online library catalogue and the CD-ROM reference systems (Butler-Pearson, 1995). Outside the United States, instructors involved in a project designed to promote learner independence encouraged students to work together through e-mail and computer conferencing without the instructor's aid (Marsh, 1997).

At the college level, the influence of student technology assistants and peer instructors reaches into classrooms, faculty offices, and computer laboratories. For example, as part of a university-wide initiative to enhance classroom instruction with multimedia technology, faculty members at Hofstra University in Hemstead, New York have been assigned student assistants with multimedia expertise (Haile, 1998). On other campuses, undergraduates have prepared faculty members to teach by offering technology workshops, including lessons on basic software applications, general personal computer knowledge, and technology integration (Sykes, 1997). The State University of New York at Stony Brook's undergraduates have been engaged as peer mentors and technology mentors for faculty (Heuer, 1997). At Pennsylvania's Gettysburg College, three tiers of student technical assistants are employed: A student "Tech Team" offers hardware and software assistance to the campus; 15 undergraduate monitors are employed to staff the computer labs, and a newly formed classroom liaison corps goes into the classroom to work with students and instructors as they use technology (Breighner, 1996;

see also http://www.gettysburg.edu/ir/response/tech.html).

The five-year, $10-million Project IMPACT (Implementing Academic Technology) at the College of Saint Benedict and Saint John's University in Minnesota has resulted in the creation of a student-staffed information technology support system, complete with an employee certification process (Lang & Bielejeski, 1998). In New Jersey, Seton Hall University's Academic Consultants for Excellence (ACEs) (http://www.tltc.shu.edu/ace/) offer a host of services to other students, including web development, assistance with a virtual learning space, technical training, in-class "Tech Buddies," computer lab staffing, and assistance with specialized courseware. A similar program is offered at William Paterson University of New Jersey (http://www.wpunj.edu/stc/) near New York City. Undergraduate peer instructors are providing tutoring online, including writing assistance in graphically rich Online Writing Labs (Anderson-Inman, 1997). At Washington State University in Pullman, Student Computing Services employs undergraduates to staff computer labs and provide training. A separate undergraduate corps, WSU's Hypernauts (described above and in the following pages), are highly trained learning-and-teaching-with-technology consultants who partner with students and faculty to design, develop, deliver, and assess innovative campus-based and distance courses.

While no means exhaustive, this list represents the breadth of services provided by undergraduate technology assistants and peer instructors. In the case of technology assistants, development of such programs may be as much out of necessity as it is borne of a belief in the intellectual and vocational benefits to students. A critical shortage in the number of available information technology professionals has begun to impact state and local agencies (Maxwell, 1998), including colleges and universities, with more severe shortages predicted for the future. According to Maxwell, the estimated average age of the information technology professional in state service is 47 years. Increasingly colleges and universities will find themselves hard pressed to compete with private industry for well-qualified information technology professionals.

A Spectrum of Services

Across the United States, most of these collegiate peer leaders are serving as technical support assistants. Their function is to collaborate with their peers as strictly technical, not pedagogical or curricular, support. At the most technical end of the spectrum are student assistants hired by information technology departments to install and troubleshoot hardware and software. At the mid-range are student assistants who build World Wide Web-based assignments to the strict specification of faculty members and those students who work in classes as technical support teaching assistants on faculty-designed assignments. At the farthest end are the more rare undergraduates who serve as independent instructors to their peers, designing assignments, creating online learning environments, and offering feedback to their peers and those students who fully partner with faculty members in the process of curricular design, decision making, and delivery. This most intensive approach is exemplified by the Washington State University Hypernauts. A lengthier discussion of this program is offered to illustrate the significant responsibility peer leaders may be, and have been, granted in integrating learning and instructional technologies.

> ...the Hypernauts' task was to infiltrate courses in which they were enrolled, introducing faculty members and fellow students to the learning possibilities of multimedia composition.

The Hypernauts Lead an Institution

In 1992, the Washington State University Hypernauts were four undergraduates and a former English instructor working on an interdisciplinary Ph.D. who toiled in a former auto-body shop in the basement of the university's College of Education building. Their work space was so cold and stark it was christened the Interactive Computer Exploration (or I.C.E.) lab. As their leader conceived it, the Hypernauts' task was to infiltrate courses in which they were enrolled, introducing faculty members and fellow students to the learning possibilities of multimedia composition. Granted partial fee waivers and academic internship credits, the Hypernauts partnered with (and guided) world civilizations and zoology instructors, English teaching assistants, and developmental educators. They reconceptualized their own and other students' traditional assignments, transforming them into multidimensional creations to challenge the mind and provoke the senses. For the most part, the work of the Hypernauts was well received; and in 1996, when named the university's teacher of the year, their zoology instructor partner gave them much of the credit for his re-energized commitment to teaching. Those who greeted the Hypernauts' work with suspicion were generally not bothered again. There was plenty of work among the "friendlies."

By 1998, the Hypernauts numbered more than 30 and were working with students from every college in the university offering undergraduate courses. They had developed three revisions of an online learning environment, or virtual classroom, had built the University's Online Writing Lab, and had served as co-instructors in the university's Freshman Seminar Program, which that year was named the best undergraduate program in the Pacific Northwest United States and one of six best internationally by the National Association of Student Personnel Administrators. The Hypernauts made presentations throughout the region, to the university's Board of Regents and Foundation members, and to major corporations. Senior Hypernauts were hired months before they graduated at salaries far outstripping those of their instructors.

The journey from 1992 to 1998 was not entirely smooth, particularly as it related to defining the task of the Hypernauts. The University was well on its way to becoming one of the most wired four-year public institutions in the country and desperately needed technical support. Would the Hypernauts provide this service as well as help their peers transform their learning experiences? Students clamoring for access to computer laboratories to word process and complete an ever-increasing number of online assignments required more computer laboratory monitors. Would the Hypernauts serve in this capacity as well as peer instruct in the Freshman Seminars? Paper and pencil-dependent faculty members now found university administrators coaxing them toward online instruction. Would the Hypernauts help build these faculty member's personal and departmental web pages, convert their assignments, and reboot their machines?

By 1999, the Hypernaut role had evolved to include: co-instruction in the WSU Freshman Seminars, curriculum redesign and development, and online mentoring. As a Freshman Seminar co-instructor, one Hypernaut is assigned to each 15-student seminar to work with students and their peer instructor as they interact in the Hypernaut-developed, web-based learning environment, the Speakeasy Studio and Café. The Hypernauts also help students develop text-based and visual theses and design end-of-term research projects. As curriculum designers and developers, the Hypernauts, employees of the University's Center for Teaching, Learning, and Technology, partner with faculty members to reconceive and rebuild their traditionally delivered courses to be offered to campus-based and distance students. As online mentors,

Hypernauts are trained to serve as writing tutors in the WSU Online Writing Lab and facilitate in online communities, including the one involving Pedro, Brenda, and other at-risk students described at the beginning of this chapter. Individual Hypernauts also occasionally contract out to faculty members (and some businesses) to enhance their web presence.

To maintain their ability to consult with and instruct faculty members and students on issues of integrating learning and instructional technologies, the Hypernauts enroll every semester in a three-credit course, variously offered under the auspices of educational psychology, educational leadership, and the Department of English. They are also responsible for reading and analyzing a substantial body of educational research, particularly with a focus on the social impact of new technologies. And they are guided to respond critically to each other's analyses of these pressing issues. Most Hypernauts work 12 to 20 hours per week in exchange for tuition waivers and time-slip pay.

Online Peer Leadership as Liberal Learning

The authors' hope is that peer leader involvement in the highly technical and mid-range technology-support oriented activities will be fairly short-lived and that peer leadership in the online environment, if it is retained, will, and should, more closely resemble the work of the Hypernauts. As colleges and universities begin to settle into the reality of the infrastructure, instructor skills, and permanent staffing needed to run wired (and wireless) institutions, they will discover permanent strategies for providing in-class technical assistance, as well as placing computers on faculty desks, installing software, and building online courses. Commercial competitors and outsourcing strategies will provide cheaper and easier solutions to many of the present infrastructure challenges. Such partnerships have already begun. Purdue University (West

Lafayette, IN), for example, is retraining its current computer skilled employees to be information technology professionals (McCollum, 1999); institutions including the College of Notre Dame (Belmont, CA) are partnering with Claris and other firms to assist students with their technology needs and to run information technology operations (Blumenstyk, 1999), and campuses across the country are collaborating with for-profit online course design firms, including E-College, Blackboard, and WebCT, to provide shrink-wrapped, web-based courses. Web masters in large, for-profit, design factories are replacing the students on campus who code for the division of continuing education or who build an individual professor's web site. While this reckoning and reorganizing may not happen tomorrow, it will happen—just as institutions learned to reinvent themselves to manage the post-World War II surge in enrollments and as hundreds discovered that Saga and Marriott could provide better food service and that Barnes and Noble could operate cost-effective bookstores.

Commercial partners and outsourcing will introduce new challenges, particularly as higher education negotiates a new identity amidst increasing pressures to balance core liberal arts values and simultaneously meet sharpened constituent expectations to develop students to meet the needs of a robust, professional workforce. What will remain is a choice to continue, or institute, the more intensive approach to integrating peer leadership and instructional technologies exemplified by the Hypernauts. As peer leaders hang up their technical support badges, individual instructors may decide they wish to retain the increased motivation, heightened sense of responsibility, and greater engagement that follow when students offer real and important responses to their peers and their institutions. These students have formed learning communities, defined by Cross (1998) as groups of people engaged in intellectual interaction for the purpose of learning. Instructors who have learned the benefits of peer lead-

ership in technology-rich environments may decide these communities should be maintained. The arguments to support their maintenance draw their strength from new thinking about epistemology, from educational research, and from pragmatism (Cross, 1998). First, these communities reflect an understanding of knowledge as a social construct; they allow students to serve "as midwife to each other person's thoughts, and each builds on the other's ideas" (Clinchy, 1990, p. 123); they connect students to each other and their faculty members around intellectual matters, and they prepare students to function in a complex economy as workers and citizens. These learning communities, with the added advantages of collaborative and cooperative learning described above, offer students a new kind of education.

If traditional non-profit institutions are not prepared to offer this new approach to learning, for-profit institutions are (Winston, 1999). These for-profits, including the University of Phoenix with its 60,000 students, DeVry with 48,000 and ITT, Education Management, and Strayer Education with their enrollments of 26,000, 19,000, and 10,000 respectively (as of early 1999), have recognized the advantages of more engaged approaches to learning, "methods students tend to prefer" (Winston, 1999, p. 16). According to University of Phoenix Vice President Swenson (1998), the free market dictates that for-profits "train" people for intellectual, not physical, work, a type of learning that these concerns believe is best accomplished in an interactive environment. "Students," Swenson suggests, "...deserve the right to learn from one another—a process that requires a teacher who can facilitate the exchange of information, ideas, and expertise" (p. 38). These for-profits are all too willing to offer this kind of learning experience and those institutions "that can't give their students the kind of education they want, when and where they want it, may wind up on the [same] beach, bypassed by new kinds of institutions that can" (Winston, p. 19). Far from being a "kind of bogeyman," these new institutions have learned from educational research and from listening to their student customers to create learning environments where (according to the University of Phoenix web site): "Students are discussing issues, sharing ideas, testing theories—essentially enjoying all of the advantages of an on-campus program, with one exception. No commute!" (qtd. in Twigg, 1998).

The complex prescription Winston suggests for competing in this new era for educators includes a shift in the relationship between institutions and their faculty, changes to faculty governance and curricular freedom, and a broadening of the range of educational "products" colleges and universities offer their students. One of these products, peer leaders who act as "Hypernauts," offer the advantages for-profits are providing students and more: an opportunity for these peer leaders to interact with other students around both academic and vocational issues, the chance to lead other students and faculty toward an understanding of the interaction between learning and technology, the occasion to hone relational and leadership skills, and the opportunity to serve others.

This service may be what distinguishes non-profit educational institutions from the new for-profit concerns. Although Swenson contends that the for-profits can, and are, offering education in the liberal tradition, the focus is, at its core, to serve the economy. The means of liberal education may be the same for both non- and for-profit, but the ends are generally not. Liberal education, according to Cronon (1999),

> nurtures human freedom in the service of the human community, which is to say that in the end it celebrates love. Whether we speak of our schools or our universities or ourselves, I hope we will hold fast to this as our constant practice, in the full depth and richness of its many meanings: Only connect. (p. 12)

It may be that all institutions, both non- and for-profit, will facilitate students' participation in a continued morphing between the concepts of community and economy. To the extent that important distinctions persist, it will be because of the non-profit sector's efforts to maintain and nurture that distinction by providing our students opportunities to identify and rise to the challenges that await them in their lives as well as their careers during and after college.

References

Anderson-Inman, L. (1997). OWLS: Online writing labs. *Journal of Adolescent & Adult Literacy, 40*(8), 650-54.

Astin, A. (1977). *Four critical years: Effects of college on beliefs, attitudes, and knowledge.* San Francisco, Jossey-Bass.

Blumenstyk, G. (1999, October 29). "Outsourcing": The results are mixed. *Chronicle of Higher Education,* A59-60.

Breighner, K. (1996). *Faculty as partners. A four-tiered training approach to the Web.* 29th Association of Small Computer Users in Education (ASCUE) Summer Conference Proceedings, North Myrtle Beach, SC.

Bruffee, K. (1995). Sharing our toys: Cooperative learning versus collaborative learning. *Change, 27,* 12-18.

Butler-Pearson, M. (1995). *Students teaching students to use the electronic information retrieval services in a high school media center.* Fort Lauderdale, FL: Nova Southeastern University.

Cabrera, A. F., Nora, A., Bernal, E. M., Terenzini, P. T., & Pascarella, E. T. (1998). Collaborative learning: Preferences, gains in cognitive & affective outcomes, and openness to diversity among college students. Annual Meeting of the Association for the Study of Higher Education, Miami, FL.

Clinchy, B. (1990). Issues of gender in teaching and learning. *Journal on Excellence in College Teaching, 1,* 52-67.

Cronon, W. (1999). Only connect: The goals of a liberal education. *Liberal Education, 85*(1), 6-12.

Cross, K. P. (1998, July/August). Why learning communities? Why now? *About Campus*, 4-11.

Dalton, J. (Ed.). (1985*). Promoting values education in student development*. (Monograph No. 4). Washington, DC: Quality of Life Research Associates.

Dey, E. (1989). *College impact and student liberalism revisited: The effect of student peers*. Los Angeles: University of California Graduate School of Education, Higher Education Research Institute.

Drucker, P. F. (1999). Beyond the information revolution. *The Atlantic Monthly*, 47-57.

Edwards, L. D., Coddington, A., & Caterina, D. (1997). Girls teach themselves, and boys too: Peer learning in a computer-based design and construction activity. *Computers & Education, 29*(1), 33-38.

Green, K. C. (1999). *Campus computing, 1998. The ninth national survey of desktop computing and information technology in American higher education*. Encino, CA: Author.

Haile, P. J. (1998). *Multimedia instruction initiative: Building faculty competence*. Annual Meeting of the American Association of Colleges for Teacher Education, New Orleans, LA.

Heuer, B. (1997). Leveraging learning through mentoring relationships. *Journal of Educational Technology Systems, 25*(2), 133-39.

Hodges, B. (1997). Task computing. *Learning and leading with technology, 25*(2), 6-12.

Ingram, T. (1998). Solving the technology support dilemma: The solution is students. *Technology Connection, 5*, 11-13.

Johnson, S. D. (1996, May/June). Technology education as the focus of research. *The Technology Teacher*, 47-49.

Johnson, D. W., Johnson, R. T., & Smith, K. A. (1998, July/August). Cooperative learning returns to college. *Change*, 27-35.

Kern, R. G. (1995). Restructuring classroom interaction with networked computers: Effects on quantity and characteristics of language production. *Modern Language Journal, 79*(4), 457-76.

Komarovsky, M. (1985). *Women in college: Shaping new feminine identities*. New York: Basic Books.

Lane, R. (1968). Political education in the midst of life's struggles. *Harvard Educational Review, 38*, 468-494.

Lang, K. J., & Bielejeski, R. (1998). *Student support that works: A solid approach*. 31st Association of Small Computer Users in Education: Proceedings of the ASCUE Summer Conference, North Myrtle Beach, SC.

Mallinckrodt, B. (1988). Student retention, social support, and dropout intention: Comparison of black and white students. *Journal of College Student Development, 29*, 60-64.

Marsh, D. (1997). Computer conferencing: Taking the loneliness out of independent learning. *Language Learning Journal, 15*, 21-25.

Maxwell, T. A. (1998). *The information technology workforce crisis: Planning for the next environment*. (NYSFIRM Government Information Focus). New York: New York State Forum for Information Resource Management.

McCollum, K. (1999, February 19). Colleges struggle to manage technology's rising costs. *Chronicle of Higher Education*, A27-30.

McInerney, V. (1996). Students' attitudes towards cooperative, self-regulated learning versus teacher directed instruction in a computer training course: A qualitative study. Annual Meeting of the American Educational Research Association, New York, NY.

Merrill, D. C., Reiser, B. J., & Landes, S. (1995). Tutoring: Guided learning by doing. *Cognition and Instruction, 13*(3), 315-372.

Merrill, D. C., Reiser, B. J., Raney, M., & Taftson, J. G. (1992). Effective tutoring techniques. A comparison of human tutors and intelligent tutoring systems. *Journal of the Learning Sciences, 2*, 277-306.

Moffatt, M. (1989). *Coming of age in New Jersey: College and American culture*. New Brunswick, NJ: Rutgers University Press.

Newcomb, T., & Wilson, E. (1966). *College peer groups*. Chicago: Aldine.

Ohta, A. S. (1995). Applying sociocultural theory to an analysis of learner discourse: Learner-learner collaborative interaction in the zone of proximal development. *Issues in Applied Linguistics, 6*(2), 93-121.

Pascarella, E. (1980). Student-faculty informal contact and college outcomes. *Review of Educational Research, 50*, 545-595.

Pascarella, E., & Terenzini, P. (1980). Student-faculty and student-peer relationships as mediators of the structural effects of undergraduate residence arrangement. *Journal of Educational Research, 73*, 344-353.

Pascarella, E., & Terenzini, P. (1981). Residence arrangement, student/faculty relationships, and freshman-year educational outcomes. *Journal of College Student Personnel, 22*, 147-156.

Peto, E., Onishi, E., & Irish, B. (1998). *Tech team: Student technology assistants in elementary & middle schools.* Worthington, OH: Linworth.

Russell, T. L. (1996). Point of view: Technology's threat to the traditional institution—real or imagined? *Journal of Continuing Education 44*(1), 22-24.

Saettler (1968). *A history of instructional technology.* New York, McGraw-Hill.

Schiewe, T. (1999, September 17). Being digital 2000. *The Chronicle of Higher Education,* A29.

Swenson, C. (1998, September/October). Customers & markets: The cuss words of academe. *Change,* 34-39.

Sykes, J. (1997). Development university style: Creating a win-win situation. *Technology Connection, 4,* 8-9.

Tucker, R. W. (1995). The virtual classroom: Quality and assessment. *Syllabus, 9*(1), 48-51.

Twigg, C. A. (1997, March/April). The promise of instructional technology: How can we reap the full benefit of new technologies? *About Campus,* 2-3.

Twigg, C. A. (1998, September/October). Unbounded liberal education: Going beyond the classroom and the campus. *About Campus,* 2-3.

Vreeland, R., & Bidwell, C. (1965). Organizational effects on student attitudes: A study of the Harvard houses. *Sociology of Education, 38*, 233-250.

Wathen, S. H., & Resnick, L. B. (1997). *Collaborative vs. individual learning and the role of explanations.* Annual Meeting of the American Educational Research Association, Chicago, IL

Winston, G. C. (1999, January/February). For-profit higher education: Godzilla or chicken little? *Change,* 13-19.

CHAPTER 7

FIRST-YEAR SEMINAR PEER LEADERS, PROGRAMS, AND PROFILES

Suzanne L. Hamid and Jayson VanHook

Given the findings that peers exert influence on each other (Astin, 1993), it is no wonder that using outstanding student role models as peer leaders is a growing trend in the first-year seminar course development in American higher education (Gardner, 1996 and Barefoot, 1997). Educators are recognizing and harnessing the potential value of employing students to facilitate learning and personal development among other students. In 1999, after witnessing the impact of peer leaders on our campus, a quest to learn more about this practice of using undergraduates as co-teachers of student success courses resulted in a collection of data from 40 peer leader programs across the U.S. (Hamid & VanHook, 1999). From this information, we were able to identify and compare a variety of peer leader programs in American higher education. The evidence seems to support the notion that *students are listening to students!*

This chapter will (a) give an overview of the data collected from 40 peer leader programs; (b) describe four peer leader programs and their related impact on retention; and (c) offer a brief profile of 16 institutions, their peer leader programs, and peer leaders.

Overview of the Results from the Peer Leader Program Questionnaire (1999)

The following information is taken from a survey on peer leadership programs conducted in 1999 (Hamid & VanHook). An invitation to present on this topic at a First-Year Experience conference served as the impetus for this study. The authors designed a survey to generate information that would introduce workshop participants to an array of issues surrounding the implementation of these programs. (See Appendix F for a copy of the questionnaire.) The questionnaire was mailed to 81 institutions, indicating on the National Resource Center for The First-Year Experience and Students in Transition's 1997 National Survey of First-Year Seminar Programs that undergraduate students were involved in instruction of first–year seminars. Forty institutions completed and returned the questionnaire.

The goal of the conference workshop mentioned above was to assist educators in creating or enhancing a peer leader program that was compatible with institutional goals and culture. Consequently, the survey asked a number of questions on the foundation, formation, and facilitation of peer leader programs with respect to rationale, administrative challenges, peer recruitment and selection, training, duties and responsibilities, financial commitments and accountability, and assessment.

An overview of the data collected on these 40 programs will be presented in the following categories: description, rationale, recruitment and selection, training, duties and responsibilities, compensation, and assessment of peer leaders. While each of these categories will highlight some specific findings, the general findings are as follows:

- « Peer leaders in first-year programs perform a variety of duties.
- « The use of peer leaders is not limited to one institutional type or size.
- « Peer leaders represent some of the best and brightest students on campuses.
- « Peer leadership is an inexpensive form of student support.
- « Peer leaders find this experience to be rewarding.

General Description

Data from this survey reflect the experiences of a total of 1,371 peer leaders who serve approximately 17,000 students. The institutions represented in this survey are of varying types and sizes. The student population for participating institutions is as follows: 19 institutions (48%) had fewer than 3,000 students; 7 institutions (18%) had between 3,000 and 10,000 students; and 13 institutions (33%) are above 10,000 in student population. The average number of peer leaders at these institutions is 35; Georgia Institute of Technology (Atlanta, GA) reported the highest number with 150 peer leaders. While the average length for program existence is 7.2 years, Bowling Green State University (Bowling Green, OH) and Fairfield University's (Fairfield, CT) programs are the oldest at 25 and 20 years old, respectively. Wide differences exist between the number of males and females; we found that more women are peer leaders than men, with 63% being women and 37% being men. Of the 40 participating institutions,

70% use sophomores in their program, 25% use juniors, and 20% use seniors. Three schools (7.5%) indicate that students from all three class levels are involved.

Rationale

One of the goals of this survey was to determine the reasons why institutions establish peer leader programs and to document the objectives of such programs. Seventeen (42.5%) of the survey respondents indicated that their programs are organized and directed by the academic affairs sector of their institution. The same number of respondents stated that their programs were organized and directed by their institutions' student affairs sector. Interestingly, despite variations in the administration of peer leader programs, the rationale for implementing these programs is consistent across institutions. The most frequently reported reasons for establishing a peer leader program are listed in descending order:

1. Peer leaders establish good connections with first-year students.
2. Peer leaders are role models for success.
3. Peer leaders serve as mentors.
4. Peer leaders can be an academic resource for students.
5. This type of program provides leadership opportunities for outstanding students.
6. A peer leader can bridge the gap between students and teacher.
7. Peer leaders can be an extension of orientation.

Recruitment and Selection of Peer Leaders

In Chapter 3, Hunter and Heath elaborate on the various criteria used by institutions for recruitment and selection of peer leaders. Most of the methods they discuss are also reported in this survey. Thirty-five of the 40 institutions reporting said they were successful in attracting students as peer leaders. A variety of methods were reported to be used to recruit peer leaders. Some of these include: letters to honor students, letters to faculty, articles in the school's newspaper, personal letters to students, teachers given the option to choose their own peer leaders, brochures and posters, letters to campus leaders, active personal contact, recommendations from current and former peer leaders, and information sessions and meetings.

Respondents report the selection of peer leaders is based on the following: faculty nominations and recommendations, a demonstration of leadership skills, grade point average, an interview by the program director, classification, submission of an essay and/or a sample lesson plan, good communication skills, enthusiasm for the course and institution, level of involvement on campus, desire to serve as a role model, and proven reliability.

We also noted that program directors use a variety of ways to match students with faculty. Some of the more frequent methods include requests to work with specific partners; matches by personality type, by gender, by academic major, by perceived strengths, or according to the student's class schedule; and matches pairing a returning peer leader with a new instructor. Some programs allow choices for teaching partner to be made based on the seniority of the students.

Training

All 40 institutions (100%) reported that they provide training for peer leaders. Many program directors indicated that while they prefer to conduct training at an off-campus site, budget constraints often prevent this from occurring. Thirty (75%) of the respondents reported that their training session(s) occurred on campus. Training formats vary to include retreats, seminars, day-long workshops, weekly seminars, and leadership courses. Consequently, the length of training also varies (see Figure 1).

Respondents were also asked to report on the types of materials used during training (see

Figure 1. *Length of Training Program for Peer Leaders* (N = 40).

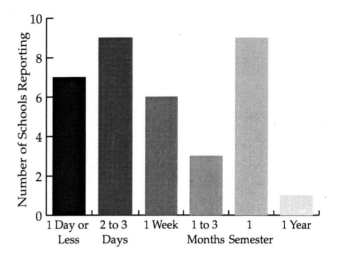

Figure 2. *Type of Supplemental Materials Used in Peer Leader Training* (N = 40).

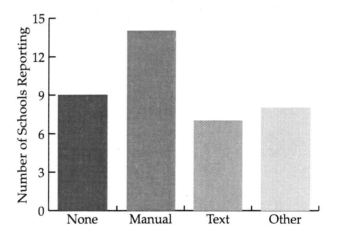

Figure 2). In general, topics covered during training are fairly consistent across institutions and include mentoring, counseling, academic advising, building relationships, leading groups, important topics within the curriculum, program objectives, conflict resolution, campus information, course agenda/manuals, coaching skills, listening skills, lesson planning, and addressing student needs.

Detailed information on recruitment, selection, and training of peer leaders is presented in Chapter 3.

Duties and Responsibilities

Survey participants were also asked to report on the goals and objectives of their peer leader programs. All responses, in varying ways, confirm that these programs are designed to facilitate student success and that peer leaders perform a variety of duties. Some of the more frequently reported responsibilities include orientation leading, teaching certain subject areas, co-teaching, facilitating ice breaker activities, planning out-of-class activities, grading papers, assisting with class discussions, organizing service-learning opportunities, weekly course planning, sending reminders to students, and conducting weekly visits with students.

> All responses, in varying ways, confirm that these programs are designed to facilitate student success and that peer leaders perform a host of duties.

Compensation

A common question among educators wanting to establish a peer leader program is, "How much do you pay these students?" Twenty of the 40 institutions reporting indicated that they awarded some form of monetary remuneration to peer leaders. Compensation includes both hourly wages and yearly stipends, ranging from $6.00 per hour to $1600 per year. Some institutions have found other creative ways to reward students. For example, Delaware Technical and Community College (Wil-mington, DE) offers a $300 bookstore scholarship while peer leaders from Georgia Institute of Technology receive free room and partial board in exchange for their services. At some institutions, remuneration for peer leaders includes a party and sweatshirt at the end of the semester, gift certificates, recognition awards, free admission to campus events, and the always coveted "awards"—moving into the residence hall early and receiving priority in housing assignment selections.

One of the more practical and popular ways to reward peer leaders, as reported in this survey, is by awarding academic credit to these students. In Chapter 3, greater attention is given to this issue, and in their chapter on leadership education, Orazem and Roller describe one example of how an academic course is facilitated at Montana State University. Other institutions like Pacific University (Forest Grove, OR), Indiana University of Pennsylvania, and the University of Maryland offer peer leaders a course for credit in return for their service to students and the institution. While these courses vary in type and number of credit hours, they all serve as a method of training and reward for peer leaders.

The survey also produced rich anecdotal evidence to support the belief that the greatest benefits for peer leaders are the intangible rewards and intrinsic satisfaction gained from serving their fellow students. The final section of this chapter describes some of these examples.

Assessment

Thirty-four of the 40 institutions in the survey reported that either students, peer leaders, and/or instructors evaluated their peer leader program. Although the methods of assessing these programs ranged from surveys to focus groups and interviews, the overall findings were consistently positive. While Fairfield University and Lee University (Cleveland, TN) reported an increase of 5% and 7% respectively in first-year to sophomore retention, the majority of institutions included only anecdotal evidence to demonstrate that the existence of their peer leader program correlates with increased retention of first-year students.

The four program descriptions in the following section are drawn from survey respondents who were able to discuss outcomes related to the peer leader program. They represent four different types of peer leader programs. Each description provides an overview of the program and describes how peer leadership correlates with the retention of first-year students at the particular institution.

Peer Leader Programs and Their Impact on Retention

University of Kentucky

Snapshot of University of Kentucky

The University of Kentucky in Lexington was founded in 1865 as a land-grant institution. Approximately 17,000 undergraduates and 7,000 graduate students are enrolled in the University's 11 colleges, five professional schools, and the Graduate School. The first-year student body is approximately 2,900, with 91% living on campus.

History and Description of UK 101

UK 101 is the University of Kentucky's first-year orientation course, cosponsored by the Dean of Undergraduate Studies Office and Student Affairs. During the 2000-01 academic year, 47 sections of the class were offered in two formats. Each year, each section of approximately 25 students is taught by an instructor (faculty member or student affairs professional) and an upperclass peer instructor.

UK 101 addresses topics such as library skills, time management, study skills, academic integrity, career exploration, university resources, campus involvement, date rape, alcohol, and diversity. Faculty and peer instructors choose additional topics such as money management and sexually transmitted diseases.

Peer Instructors

Since UK 101's inception in 1989, the peer instructor position has been a cornerstone of the course. Applicants must have attained junior or senior classification and have earned at least a 3.0 GPA. Peer instructors are selected based on their applications and interviews. Attention

is given to each applicant's leadership experience, academic record, and time availability. All peer instructors participate in a two-day training workshop, and they maintain contact with the student affairs UK 101 administrator throughout the duration of the class via e-mails, phone calls, and meetings.

The peer instructors' role has evolved over the years from a "student assistant" to a "co-instructor." Peer instructors devote approximately seven hours a week toward the class. Expectations and responsibilities include the following:

« Meet regularly with instructor to plan class sessions and peer instructor's role in each session, discuss progress of course and students, and provide feedback to instructor
« Call guest presenters several days in advance of class to discuss peer instructor's role in class
« Read or evaluate student journals and other assignments
« Prepare and make announcements about upcoming campus events, student organizations, important dates and deadlines, etc.
« Offer campus tours during the first week of classes
« Assist students in setting up e-mail accounts
« Facilitate session on alcohol use
« Lead tour of library and assist students with library assignments
« Conduct tour of career center and assist students with online career exploration exercises
« Reinforce points made in class and share personal experiences and examples when appropriate
« Converse with students before and after class and have follow-up conversations with students about their exams, any concerns, etc.
« Respond to all e-mail messages and phone calls from students
« Make time for impromptu lunches or snack breaks with students in the class
« Plan a social event with the class (Each section is provided $50 for a social.)
« Act as a role model and mentor

« Follow-up with students by phone or e-mail after the course ends

Results of UK 101

Faculty and student evaluations are overwhelmingly positive to UK 101. More than 90% of students who take UK 101 recommend it to incoming students. Furthermore, as shown in Table 1 below, institutional research indicates that retention rates are higher for students in UK 101 than for those not enrolled.

Table 1. *Fall to Fall Retention Rates of First-Year Students, UK*

	1995	1996	1997	1998
Enrolled in UK 101	83.3%	82.5%	84.8%	82.2%
Not enrolled in UK 101	78.7%	78.6%	79.1%	78.7%

Written evaluations by the first-year students suggest the use of peer instructors is one of the contributing factors to the success of UK 101. Remarks such as, "It's great having a student instructor who has actually been there and knows what we are talking about." are not uncommon. The peer instructors are reported to be both credible and helpful to first-year students. Year after year, more than 99% of the UK 101 students rate their peer instructors as helpful or very helpful. The faculty instructors also praise the peer instructors for their contributions to the class as exemplified in the following statement: "My peer instructor was a rock... students related well to him. He gave good advice and had more inherent credibility than any of the speakers, including me!"

Given these results, administrators at the University of Kentucky indicate they will continue to place a high priority on the role of UK 101 peer instructors.

For more information, contact:
Rebecca Jordan
University of Kentucky

Southwest Missouri State University

Snapshot of Southwest Missouri State University

The University was founded in 1905 as the Fourth District Normal School and became Southwest Missouri State Teachers College in 1919. Further growth and development resulted in the name being changed to Southwest Missouri State University (SMSU) in 1972. Today, the institution is a multipurpose, three-campus university system providing instruction, research, and service programs for both urban and rural environments. Enrollment at the Springfield campus in Fall 2000 included 15,423 undergraduates and 2,423 graduate students. Of the 3,540 first-year students, approximately 2,400 are enrolled in the first-year success course (IDS 110).

History and Description of IDS 110

IDS 110 Introduction to University Life started in Fall 1994 as a one-credit hour, graded course offered by the Department of Continuous Orientation. Each of the 100 sections has a maximum of 25 students and is taught by faculty, staff, and graduate students. Continuous Orientation also supports the peer leadership course, IDS 310.

The Continuous Orientation Program (IDS 110 and IDS 310) helps to unite students in support groups, motivate involvement in the campus community, provide large-group presentations on health and safety issues, and encourage responsible citizenship. IDS 110 topics include academic planning, library orientation, the value of college, study skills, test anxiety, career planning, health/wellness/

safety, diversity, stress management, money management, campus and community involvement, speaking and writing, campus resources, critical thinking, understanding professors, relationships, group building, social skills, and values clarification.

Peer Leadership

In Fall 1995, the peer leadership component was initiated along with a course IDS 310 Peer Leadership. The class size is limited to 20 students per section. Applicants must have attained sophomore status along with a minimum GPA of 3.0. Peer leaders pay the IDS 310-course tuition up front, but at midterm they receive a tuition reimbursement. Of the 55 to 65 peer leaders who serve each academic year, approximately one third are males and two thirds are females. Peer leaders are expected to be dependable and punctual, show enthusiasm for the University, take initiative in work, have positive attitudes, be honest and trustworthy, uphold the IDS 110 course requirements and standards, communicate effectively in speaking and in writing, be organized, have good time management skills, maintain confidentiality, and be an example in personal appearance and conduct.

The Associate Dean of University College directs the peer leadership program for Continuous Orientation. A mental health clinician from the Counseling and Testing Center participates in the IDS 310 classes and assists with the training workshops of both teachers and peer leaders. Each IDS 310 section is a support group for the respective peer leaders.

Assessment

Peer leaders report their greatest satisfaction with the experience comes from helping students, becoming acquainted and working with the lead teacher, assisting with class activities and teaching, making new friends, and developing positive relationships with students (i.e. making a difference in the lives of first-year students and seeing progress in their adjustment to college).

What do they learn about themselves by being peer leaders? Students respond most frequently by saying that they enjoyed helping and working with people, enjoyed leading class activities and discussions, and gained more confidence in speaking to groups. In addition, other responses indicate that peer leadership experiences confirmed or changed the students' minds about their major, provided effective interaction with the teacher and students, improved interpersonal skills, and helped them to handle a busy schedule and better manage their time.

> ...other responses indicate that peer leadership experiences confirmed or changed the students' minds about their major, ... improved interpersonal skills, and helped them to handle a busy schedule and better manage their time.

According to peer leaders, the most effective aspects of the peer leadership program include the following: meeting with other peer leaders, sharing experiences (e.g., effective techniques, helpful resources, and problem solving), making new friends, having a positive support system, networking, and developing leadership skills.

Impact of Peer Leadership on First-Year Success Rates

One possible indicator of the success of the peer leader program is the higher first-year student to sophomore retention rate of IDS 110—or the honors-equivalent—participants over nonparticipants. Institutional research has indicated that retention rates are higher for students in IDS 110 and UHC 110 (Honors) than for all first-year students, as shown below in Table 2.

Table 2. *Retention Rates for First-Year Students at SMSU*

	1995	1996	1997	1998	1999
Enrolled in IDS/UHC 110	NA	76.4%	77.4%	78.0%	81.1%
Not enrolled in IDS/UHC 110	62.4%	66.8%	66.9%	68.7%	72.1%

Among the most valuable reported aspects of the IDS 110 course and program are its character-building components, which help students develop a strong sense of personal and civic responsibility. As evidence of this strong emphasis on character, the first-year program at SMSU was recognized in *The Templeton Guide: Colleges That Encourage Character Development* in October 1999.

For more information contact:
Mona Casady
Southwest Missouri State University

University of the Pacific

Snapshot of University of the Pacific

Pioneer Methodist ministers established the University of the Pacific in 1851 as the first chartered institution of higher learning in California. Today, UOP is a private university with a main campus in Stockton, California; a professional School of Law in Sacramento, and a professional School of Dentistry in San Francisco. Approximately 4,000 students are enrolled at the main Stockton campus. About half of the students live on or near campus. The first-year student class size is approximately 700. UOP is an ethnically diverse school, composed of about 60% white, non-Hispanic students; 30% Asian-American students; and 10% African-American, Native-American, and Hispanic students. For about 20% of the students, their native language is not English.

History and Description of Student Advising and Retention Services Programs

The Student Advising Program was founded at the University of the Pacific in 1974. Traditionally, student advisors have worked with various student life programs to provide peer support. These support programs include international student services, admissions, services for adult learners, and Crossroads (the substance abuse prevention program). Later in 1997, the Office of Retention Services was created. This is a "one-stop office" where students can receive tutoring, study skills sessions, financial aid counseling, career counseling, or personal counseling. Professors are asked to refer students who are absent excessively or doing less than satisfactorily in their classes. Once a student is referred, peer retention student advisors contact the referred student and make further appropriate referrals. The offices of Student Advising and Retention Services work closely with student advisors to serve as the method of program and service delivery.

The Office of Retention Services also produces the Program of Academic Support Services (PASS). PASS targets at-risk students at their entry to the university and throughout their performance in school. PASS provides a way for students to keep in contact with a peer student advisor or retention student advisor, in order to make sure these students are receiving the tutoring, study skills workshops, or other university services.

Peer Advisors

Forty-five undergraduate peer advisors receive training as paraprofessional members of the student life staff. These student advisors work with entering students beginning with summer orientation programs and concluding officially at the end of their first year on campus. Each student advisor works with 24 to 36 new students, assisting them with academic and personal adjustment. Student advisors work with a faculty-advising partner to provide assistance with course selection and registration and, when appropriate, refer students to other campus resources.

All student advisors are selected through a comprehensive process in the fall semester that includes academic screening, group and individual interviews, and recommendations from faculty and student advisors. Those selected attend a training course during the spring semester. Core course work includes sessions on Chickering's student development theory, active listening, class demonstrations, and crisis counseling. Additionally, student advisors receive instruction in confidentiality and professionalism, the new student profile, one-to-one and group delivery models of academic support and intervention, study strategy content areas (e.g., time management, reading and study systems, test taking, and motivation), responsibilities of working with their faculty advisor partner, academic rules and regulations, student life resources, and referral techniques.

A group of eight student advisors is also selected to work directly with the Office of Retention Services. They provide the outreach component by making the initial contact with students who are referred and explain the services that are available. Retention student advisors provide one-on-one peer mentoring, study strategy counseling, and referral to other campus services. Retention student advisors also work as peer mentors in the Program of Academic Support Services (PASS) so that each PASS participant is not only connected with services but also is assisted with academic and personal adjustment.

Assessment

The Office of Retention Services performs biannual, formative assessments of its referral system and its PASS program using qualitative and quantitative methods. For example, analysis of survey data showed that PASS students more often referred to the helpfulness and support of the retention student advisors and the general student advisors than to the actual services received. Examples of student remarks about the PASS program are as follows:

> The PASS staff members "encourage me to use tutors, talk to my professors and pay attention to my grades, so I am doing better."

> "I have acquired better study skills and better time management."

As shown in Table 3 below, UOP has seen an increase in the rate of first-year student to sophomore retention by more than 6% in the last five years, which correlates with the existence of its peer leader program.

In conclusion, administrators indicate that the peer mentoring provided to students at UOP could be the strongest aspect of the services of the Office of Retention Services and the Student Advising Center. The scope of the outreach of these two programs continues to grow as improvements are made.

For more information contact:
Sandra Mahoney
University of the Pacific

Table 3. *First-Year to Sophomore Retention Rates, UOP*

	1994-95	1995-96	1996-97	1997-98	1998-99
All first-year students	81.4%	82.1%	83.8%	85.7%	87.4%

State University of West Georgia

Snapshot of the State University of West Georgia

Located in Carrollton, Georgia, the State University of West Georgia (SUWG) campus is positioned in the rolling hills of the southern Appalachian Mountains, 50 miles west of Atlanta. SUWG is a regional university within the State of Georgia system. Total enrollment of the University is approaching 10,000 students (81% undergraduate). In Fall 2000, the University welcomed more than 1,500 incoming first-year students. Most of these students are enrolled full-time and live on campus. The minority population is 24% of the larger population, with African Americans being the largest group.

History and Description of Peer Leadership at SUWG

The Freshman Center at the SUWG offers first-year students a three-pronged peer leadership/mentoring program: first-year student and HOPE scholar mentoring, minority peer mentoring, and peer-led classroom workshops. Each mentoring subprogram is coordinated by Freshman Center staff and shares fundamental characteristics in training and programming. All programs recruit, train, and support sophomore and other upperclass students who essentially serve as big brothers/sisters or instructional facilitators to the first-year students. These first-year students usually sign up at summer or fall orientation sessions to be a part of the mentoring or academic workshop programs.

HOPE and First-Year Student Mentoring

The state of Georgia offers all high school graduates who have completed a college preparatory curriculum and who have maintained B averages a full tuition and fees scholarship to any state college or university. These HOPE Scholars must maintain a B average in their college courses to keep their scholarships. Unfortunately, nearly 3 out of 4 HOPE scholars statewide lose their scholarships at the end of their first year. For this reason, the HOPE Scholar Mentoring Program was created at SUWG three years ago. This program enlists and trains HOPE scholars who have "kept their HOPE" past the end of the first-year GPA checkpoint. Coupled with the HOPE Scholarship Mentoring Program, the Freshman Center offers a peer mentor to students who are neither HOPE Scholars nor minority students but who are interested in having a peer mentor. These mentors assist first-year students with orientation. They further provide important sources of information about the communities of Carrollton and Atlanta, campus social events, support services on campus, and general who-what-where-when-how information.

Minority Peer Mentoring

The Minority Peer Mentoring Program enlists the aid of sophomore, junior, and senior students of color to provide a nurturing relationship to first-year SUWG students of color and to help them make a successful transition to university life. The peer mentor program provides the opportunity for mentors to have a positive impact on students while developing their leadership, communication, and teamwork skills. Program administrators say these mentors serve as guides, resources, and role models to first-time students who might otherwise have a negative experience due to feelings of confusion, isolation, and discouragement because of their minority status.

Workshop Peer Leaders

The peer-led team learning workshop model incorporates a coalition of faculty, students, and learning specialists or student services professionals. This model provides an active learning experience for students, creates a leadership role for undergraduates, and engages faculty in a creative new dimension in teaching. The model is particularly useful for large introductory courses in which new students tend to feel lost. Following the lecture component of a course, peer leaders meet with groups of six to eight students for two hours each week, and under their guidance, the group works its way through a set of challenging problems or discussion questions prepared by the instructor.

The peer leaders meet weekly with the course instructor and sometimes a learning specialist or student services professional to discuss the practical aspects of leading small groups. They are introduced to strategies for fostering collaborative learning and, almost as a by-product, gain an expanded understanding of and appreciation for both the discipline and the intricacies of good interpersonal skills. Often, first-year student participants become peer leaders their second year in school.

Faculty members take part in arranging the workshop environment, selecting the materials, and interacting with the workshop leaders. The mentoring relationship that faculty members establish with leaders serves as an important model for peer leaders to follow as they develop a relationship with their first-year student group members.

Initiation of Leadership Course

After the recruitment and selection of peer mentors for the various peer leadership programs, the leaders are required to take either a short-term, but intensive training seminar or a course for credit entitled, "What Do You Really Know About Leadership?" This course has been included in the general education curriculum and combines a theoretical study of leadership with an experiential component. Course credit acts as a reward for those student leaders who do not receive financial compensation.

Results of the Mentoring Program

All programs have demonstrated an increased rate of retention and college satisfaction for all participants, both mentors and mentees. Grades are consistently higher by one half to a full letter grade for participants in the peer workshop program when compared with other students of similar characteristics in the same class. The attention and information given the HOPE Scholars have increased their rate of maintaining the scholarship. The minority mentoring program has a first-year to sophomore retention rate that is more than 10% higher than the larger population. Given these results, the Freshman Center, with the support of the larger university, is seeking to expand these programs to reach an even larger proportion of the first-year class.

For more information, contact:
Cheryl Rice
State University of West Georgia

Program Synopses and Peer Comments

This final section provides profiles of 16 peer leader programs. The profiles are drawn from institutions that responded to the Peer Leader Program Questionnaire and that gave permission to identify their institution with their responses. The profiles provide a brief description of the institution, the date when the program was established, the number of peer leaders involved in the program, and a comment on the experience from a peer leader. Many also include information on the number of students served, program selection criteria, and types of compensation provided. The peer leader comments provide anecdotal evidence about the benefits of these experiences for the leaders themselves. Some of the benefits identified by peer leaders include:

« Personal satisfaction that comes from helping others

« Development of transferable and marketable skills such as communication, problem-solving, creativity, analytical, and critical thinking skills
« Opportunities to learn more about themselves
« Opportunities for personal growth
« Increased understanding of their own learning processes

The institutions represented here include public and private, secular and religious, large and small colleges and universities.

BOWLING GREEN STATE UNIVERSITY   Bowling Green, Ohio

*Bowling Green is a liberal arts institution offering 200
degree programs. The current enrollment is 18,900.*

Peer Leader Program:

« Established in 1974
« 750 students are enrolled in first-year seminar program.
« 25 peer leaders
« Peer leaders are trained in seminars conducted throughout the spring and summer.
« Peer leaders receive a stipend of $1500.

For more information, contact:

Jodi Webb
Director, First Year Experience Program

Peer Response:

Working in this leadership position with my peers encouraged me to become a strong role model for them. I was motivated to demonstrate appropriate behavior and inspired to guide them in a positive direction. I was not only able to build strong relationships with several students, but I also built a partnership with my course instructor. She gave me a strong sense of ownership within the course and always made me feel that my role was critical for the success of the students. The position gave me a strong connection to the University and enhanced my experience permanently.—*Rebecca Nieto*

CONCORDIA UNIVERSITY   Mequon, Wisconsin

*Concordia University is a private, four-year liberal arts
institution. Serving 4,100 students, Concordia offers 37 majors
of study, while maintaining a teacher-student ratio of 17:1.*

Peer Leader Program:

« Established in 1995
« Uses 11 peer leaders; eight carry senior status
« Peer leaders must maintain a minimum
   GPA of 3.0.
« Peer leaders are matched through interviews
   with the first-year seminar instructors.
« Peer leaders receive a stipend of $1500.

For more information, contact:

John Beck
Director, Freshman Year Experience

Peer Response:

There is no cause more worthwhile in life than helping other people. At a college campus, freshmen are often those students that need the most help. As a peer leader I have seen students struggle with homesickness, pregnancy, forceful coaches, hostile roommates, death, and more. Freshmen have to deal with all of these issues while trying to adjust to an entirely new way of life. There are so many benefits to being a peer leader, but my favorite is providing hope for students that need a light at the end of the tunnel.—*Heather Batt*

EASTERN COLLEGE   St. Davids, Pennsylvania

Eastern College was founded in 1932. It is a coeducational, private, four-year institution. Student enrollment is currently 2,400.

Peer Leader Program:

« Piloted in 1993
« 375 students are enrolled in the first-year seminar program.
« 16 peer leaders
« Peer leaders enroll in a two-hour credit course.
« Peer leaders receive a $300 stipend.

For more information, contact:

Laurie A. Schreiner
Professor and Chair of Psychology

Peer Response:

I have served as a peer leader to first-year students for three years. In this program, incoming students deal with world-views, racial reconciliation, justice, and many other issues that come along when living in the community. In addition, this program helps in the personal and academic development of each student through goal setting, self-assessment, and the exploration of a college major. As a peer leader, I have witnessed the transformation of many students. I have had the priceless experience of watching many of these students blossom into well-rounded, confident, successful individuals.—*Jeanine Harris*

EMMANUEL COLLEGE   Franklin Springs, Georgia

Emmanuel was founded in 1919. Over 1,600 students attend this private, four-year liberal arts college.

Peer Leader Program:

« Established in 1995
« 20 peer leaders
« 300 students are enrolled in the first-year seminar program.
« Peer leaders volunteer for this position and are matched to the faculty by the academic dean.

For more information, contact:

Cindy Luper
Director, Career Services

Peer Response:

While at times my position has been challenging and has stretched my abilities, it is this same refining of my character which I have come to appreciate and seek. Helping other students find themselves in the academic and social spheres of college and facilitating their success in those vital areas has been a real joy. As I aid in their educational success, I am receiving an education. Leadership skills, negotiation abilities, and a counselor's heart have been developed within me. In this highly demanding world of 'reality,' of which college students are so often far removed, there will be a premium placed on individuals who possess these desirable traits and are able to develop them in other people.—*Mike Shin*

FAIRFIELD UNIVERSITY   Fairfield, Connecticut

*Fairfield University is an independent, Roman Catholic
liberal arts college. The teacher-student ratio is 13:1,
serving 4,500 students.*

Peer Leader Program:

« Established in 1992
« 120 peer leaders
« Application process includes paper application, interview, and a group interview
« Students volunteer for the position

For more information, contact:

Timothy P. Lloyd
Director, New Student Programs

Peer Response:

The First-Year Experience Program at Fairfield is an amazing way to become involved in peer leadership. This program helps to smooth the difficult transition that students go through when they leave high school and enter the world of college. The personal fulfillment that I have received by being in this program has been astonishing. It is a wonderful feeling to know that you have made a difference in the lives of incoming students. While working on the program, I learned how to be a dedicated and diligent leader and have acquired new skills that will stay with me long after my college experience has ended.—*Cori Martindale*

GENEVA COLLEGE   Beaver Falls, Pennsylvania

*Geneva College is a Christian liberal arts institution.
Current enrollment is around 2,000. Thirty-five degrees of
study are offered.*

Peer Leader Program:

« Established in 1990
« 400 students are enrolled in the first-year seminar program.
« 66 peer leaders
« Peer leaders receive a stipend of $250.

For more information, contact:

Joy M. Jewell
Vice President, Student Development

Peer Response:

My experience at Geneva College as part of the leadership staff for fall orientation has taught me what it means to be a true servant leader for the kingdom of Christ. I had the opportunity to mentor staff members while meeting and interacting with incoming students. My responsibilities as part of the leadership staff have helped me discover my own strengths and weaknesses.—*Ann Ramsey*

INDIANA UNIVERSITY OF PENNSYLVANIA   Indiana, Pennsylvania

*Indiana University was founded in 1875. Approximately
14,000 students are currently enrolled.*

Peer Leader Program:

« Established in 1984
« 12 peer leaders
« Serves 350 students in the first-year seminar program
« Training is a spring semester class.

For more information, contact:

Cassandra C. Green
*Coordinator, Peer Leader Advisors Program/
Learning Center*

Peer Response:

I consider my experience as a peer advisor in the learning center program at IUP to be a beautiful experience. I looked up to my peer advisor, and I enjoy my advisees looking up to me. I also enjoy it when my former students return, expressing to me the impact I have had on their lives. This is one of the best jobs I ever had!—***Quincy Booth***

LEE UNIVERSITY   Cleveland, Tennessee

*Lee University is a private, Christian, four-year liberal arts
college. It has the second largest undergraduate enrollment of
Tennessee's private institutions with 3,259 students.*

Peer Leader Program:

« Piloted in 1995
« 700 students are enrolled in the first-year seminar program.
« 36 peer leaders
« Training includes three days of interaction with faculty and staff.
« Peer leaders must have a minimum GPA of 3.5.

For more information, contact:

Suzanne Hamid
Director, First-Year Programs

Peer Response:

Not only was I able to use the experience as a resume builder, but it actually became the center of my discussion at an interview I had for medical school. My interviewer spent 20 minutes during a one-hour interview discussing the responsibilities of being a peer leader. He was impressed that I was chosen for such a program and was equally impressed that in my last year, I chose to help new students with whatever advice I could give to them.—***Emanuel Cocian***

OREGON STATE UNIVERSITY   Corvallis, Oregon

Oregon State is a public institution serving 15,000 students.
The university offers 200 different degree programs to its
students.

Peer Leader Program:

« Established in 1998
« 65 peer leaders
« 1,350 students are enrolled in the first-year
   seminar program.
« Peer leaders receive credit in the form of a
   teaching internship.

For more information, contact:

Jackie Balzar
Coordinator, First Year Experience

Peer Response:

Being a peer leader offers many wonderful
opportunities. I do think it is a great resume
builder, and it helps your speaking skills as
you teach in front of a medium size group. The
main reason why I keep coming back as a peer
leader is because I know that I am helping new
students at OSU feel this is the place for them.
I still see some of my students that I helped
and feel satisfied that they are succeeding in
their college careers and completing their
goals.—*Gloria E. Adams*

PACIFIC UNIVERSITY   Forest Grove, Oregon

Pacific University was founded as a private school in 1849.
It is a four-year liberal arts college serving 1,800 students.

Peer Leader Program:

« Established in 1994
« 300 students are enrolled in the first-year
   seminar program.
« 13 peer leaders
« Four hours of academic credit are awarded
   to peer leaders.

For more information, contact:

P. W. Beard
Director, Academic Coordination

Peer Response:

When I think about my FYS mentoring experience, my sense of responsibility seems im-
mense. I wanted very badly to extend to my
students the care that other people at Pacific
had given to me. My function was, in many
ways, to serve as a conduit. As their FYS mentor, I felt I was a pretty important lens through
which my students could see possibility those
first few weeks.—*Becky Ball*

SHORTER COLLEGE   Rome, Georgia

Shorter is a private institution dedicated to public service.
Current enrollment is 1,800 students.

Peer Leader Program:

« Established in 1992
« 10 to 15 peer leaders
« 290 students enrolled in the first-year seminar program.
« Peer leaders earn two hours of academic credit.
« Peer leaders receive a $100 stipend.

For more information, contact:

Charlotte Davis
Vice President, Student Development

Peer Response:

I remember what it was like to be a freshman, the questions I had, the anxieties I felt, and the fears I faced. I also remember looking up to and respecting those upperclassmen who were ready and willing to answer my questions, calm my anxieties, and diminish my fears. I believe that it is for these reasons that I decided to become a peer leader. I wanted to become what so many others had been for me. This experience has given me an incredible opportunity to learn more about my school and myself while helping others.—***Christine Hojdila***

UNIVERSITY OF KENTUCKY   Lexington, Kentucky

The University of Kentucky offers 98 degrees to more than
30,000 students. Studies include both undergraduate and
graduate levels.

Peer Leader Program:

« Founded in 1989
« More than 1,000 students are enrolled in the first-year seminar program.
« 44 peer leaders
« Peer leaders may serve in the eight-week training course or the full-semester course.

For more information, contact:

Rebecca Jordan
Director, New Student Programs

Peer Response:

I suspect that many peer leaders, myself included, assume such roles to gain experience and to build resumes. Somewhere throughout the process, however, an amazing thing happens. Call it self-fulfillment. Becoming a peer leader enabled me to grow as a person because it taught me that by helping others, I was helping myself. I know that being a peer leader will greatly benefit me when I begin my career. I will be successful in working with others, solving problems, and being an initiator and innovator. What I am even more sure of is what will come at the end of the day: self-pride, respect, knowledge, and contentment. I have made a difference.—***Angie Bryant***

UNIVERSITY OF MARYLAND   College Park, Maryland

The University of Maryland was founded in 1856. Current
enrollment is more than 25,000.

Peer Leader Program:

« Established in 1995
« 35 peer leaders
« 700 students are served by the first-year seminar program.
« Peer leaders earn four credit hours.

For more information, contact:

Matthew R. Wawrzynski
Assistant Director, First-Year Student Programs
and Research

Peer Response:

Being an undergraduate teaching assistant has allowed me to analyze critically my own experiences and help other students deal with transitional issues and challenges. I have been able to gain a better understanding of my own learning by actively engaging in the learning process of others. Learning is no longer a distant concept. In fact, in addition to the weekly lessons I learned while teaching, this experience has been my most rewarding academic pursuit.—***Kelly A. Kish***

UNIVERSITY OF MINNESOTA   Duluth, Minnesota

The University of Minnesota currently serves 8,000
students. Undergraduates may choose from 11 bachelor
degrees in 70 majors.

Peer Leader Program:

« Established in 1995
« 800 students are enrolled in program.
« 28 peer leaders
« Course credit is given to all peer leaders.

For more information, contact:

Paula Knudson
First Year Experience Director

Peer Response:

I feel like I'm truly helping students. I feel responsible and mature and loved being part of an important asset of UMD.—***Allison Jorgensen***

I really enjoy answering students' questions and letting them know I am a resource for them while at the same time learning about myself.—***Wes Griffith***

UNIVERSITY OF MONTANA   Missoula, Montana

The University of Montana is a public institution. There are
13,000 students currently enrolled.

Peer Leader Program:

« Established in 1980
« 80 to 90 peer leaders
« 2,000 students are served by the first-year seminar program.
« Academic credit is given to all peer leaders.

For more information, contact:

S. Melanie Hoell
Director, University College

Peer Response:

Because of my experiences, I have learned how to listen actively and how to convey vital information to others. I have learned how to give advice, make referrals, and sort out problems with respect to a student's success in higher education. My analytical, critical thinking, and communication skills have truly bloomed. I have grown personally and professionally, made many new friends, and gained an incredible entourage of mentors who guide the program. The act of helping others has been heartwarming and gratifying. This program has been my home away from home the past four years.—*Jody Sullivan*

UNIVERSITY OF SOUTH CAROLINA   Columbia, South Carolina

The University of South Carolina is a public liberal arts
institution. 26,000 students are currently enrolled.

Peer Leader Program:

« Established in 1993
« More than 2,000 students are enrolled in the first-year seminar program.
« 100 peer leaders
« Three hours of graduate level credit are awarded to peer leaders.

For more information, contact:

Dan Berman
Director, University 101

Peer Response:

Being involved in the peer leader program has opened so many doors for me to grow not only as a student but also as a person. My involvement in our University 101 class has been an open opportunity to learn more about myself, and to learn more about the freshman of today as compared to when I started college, only two years ago. Also, being involved as a peer leader has given me a chance to really explore what campus life at USC has to offer. This program has made me a more well-rounded student.—*Ashlon A. Landgley*

References

Astin, A. W. (1993). *What matters in college? Four critical years revisited.* San Francisco: Jossey-Bass.

Barefoot, B. O. (1997). *National survey of first-year seminar programs* [Unpublished summary]. Columbia, SC: University of South Carolina, National Resource Center for The First-Year Experience and Students in Transition. Retrieved January 22, 2001 from the World Wide Web: http://www.sc.edu/fye/resources/surveys/survey97.htm.

Gardner, J. N. (1996). Power to peer. *Keystone Newsletter.* Belmont, CA: Wadsworth Publishing Company.

Hamid, S. L., & VanHook, J., (1999). *Peer leader program questionnaire* [Unpublished raw data]. (Available from the Office of First-Year Programs, Lee University, Cleveland, TN, 37320-3450).

CHAPTER 8

SUMMARY AND RECOMMENDATIONS

Suzanne L. Hamid and John N. Gardner

We have seen confirmed throughout this monograph that peer leadership has been practiced on college and university campuses for decades. Moreover, peer leaders and peer leadership programs act as buffers and safety nets and serve any number of other important metaphorical functions throughout the varying stages of our students' collegiate journeys. Peers are often the ones who slow the leaks in the education pipeline. They facilitate seamless transitions for their peers. They can make the work of educators easier. In serving their peers and their institutions, they are leaders in their own right!

When we decided to do a monograph on peer leadership, we knew that complete coverage of all the uses of this term was not possible. Furthermore, although the literature of higher education is replete with theoretical support for this concept, we were fully aware that there was a dearth of information on how this practice, in all its manifestations, was being implemented on campuses. Throughout the preceding chapters, the authors have attempted to correct this deficiency. What then have we learned from this monograph?

Summary of Findings

1. A wealth of empirical evidence exists in the literature of higher education to support the notion that students influence each other. The impact of students on the academic and social development of their peers has been well established. The programs and practices described here build on this foundational knowledge.

2. There are many descriptors for students who help students on college campuses. These terms include peer leader, peer educator, student assistant, peer helper, student mentor, and student aide.

3. In their roles as paraprofessionals, students deliver a variety of services to their fellow students. Arguably, these services not only have educational value but also are highly cost-effective. However, the empirical evidence supporting the cost-effectiveness of such delivery models has yet to be systematically gathered.

4.   Institutions of all types, sizes, and selectivity use peer leaders on their campuses. For example, both four-year and two-year institutions administer peer leader programs. Some community college educators resist the idea of developing peer leader programs because they do not believe they have students who are "advanced." But given the exceptional maturity, goal orientation, intelligence, and experience in higher education of many community college students, we believe a large cohort of very able students exists on these campuses who would make outstanding role models for entering community college students.

5.   Peer leaders are at work both within the classroom and beyond, and they represent some of our campuses' most academically talented students.

6.   While overwhelmingly peer leader programs are designed to assist the entire cohort of new students, some peer leader programs focus on the needs of special student populations such as minority or underprepared students.

7.   Peer leaders are compensated for their work in a variety of ways; two of the most common are monetary compensation and/or academic credit from a course designed to support their work as peer leaders.

8.   Essential to the successful operation of any program is the formalization of such basic practices as goal setting for involved faculty, staff, and peer leaders, training for all, and the development of contracts which spell out the responsibilities of members of the teams.

9.   Institutions report having fewer male peer leaders than females. This mirrors widespread patterns of under-representation of males in service roles on campus, in particular, and in co-curricular activities, in general. The reasons for this merit concern and attention from all higher educators as we strive to see both men and women serve others and achieve success during their college careers.

10. While peer leader training can be achieved in a variety of ways, the two most common forms are credit-bearing academic courses taken prior to or during the peer leading experience and/or training in non-credit workshop settings.

11. There is widespread anecdotal evidence, based on self-reports from peer leaders, that their experiences helping other students are very rewarding.

12. Students are more likely to embrace new technologies more quickly and more readily than are some members of the faculty. Similarly, in the case of peer leader programs, peer leader facility with new technologies has a positive impact on the attitudes and skills of other students and faculty members.

Recommendations and Implications for Future Practice

1.   We urge educators who read this volume to seek multiple ways to inform fellow campus personnel about the rationale and history of using student leaders to achieve successful academic and social integration for fellow undergraduates, especially first-year students.

2.   While lauding the virtues of peer leaders, institutions and programs using them must remember that they are paraprofessionals; they must have significant training, support, and clearly defined contractual limits and expectations.

3.   Peer leaders' accomplishments must be validated and celebrated. It is not sufficient to simply pay them. Yet the question of compensation needs to receive careful consideration from program developers. We believe that all too frequently an argument for not attempting some kind of new program is the justifiable concern that financial resources are difficult to find. Monetary compensation for peer leaders would be such a resource consideration. But in light of the fact that many

programs use students who are not financially compensated, this issue does not have to be an insurmountable hurdle. On the other hand, there is some evidence to suggest that monetary compensation may not always be the best or most effective motivator. Student focus groups conducted at the University of South Carolina to ascertain student leaders' willingness to serve as peer leaders urged developers of the peer leader program not to provide monetary compensation for students. These students feared that monetary compensation would contaminate the motivation of future peer leaders. Neither of these positions is an argument against any compensation or an argument for exploiting students who perform significant services on our campuses. It is, quite simply, an argument to carefully consider alternative forms of "compensation."

4.   In the spirit of the challenging questions raised in Chapter 1, we recommend that developers of future programs consider these key questions:

« By what criteria and what process should we select peer leaders?

« How will we provide appropriate training and ongoing support for peer leaders?

« How do we wish first-year students to be different as a result of having interacted with peer leaders?

« How can we collect evidence on the effectiveness of such interventions?

« What are the key mission-driven values your institution wants to see illustrated and reinforced through the peer leadership program?

5.   Program directors must make efforts to prepare appropriate policy statements, handbooks, and manuals for everyone involved in peer leader programs. These should outline processes and procedures to ensure accountability of peer leaders, faculty and administrative teaching partners, and program administrators. Training of peer leaders should include such issues as prescribing limits and boundaries and developing and honoring faculty/staff/peer leader contracts.

6.   We strongly recommend institutions set high standards for the selection of peer leaders so that entering undergraduates are exposed not only to students who are socially successful and adept, but more importantly, to students who have been academically successful.

7.   We recommend that peer leaders be involved in the processes of recruitment, selection, and training of future peer leaders.

8.   We recommend that to the fullest extent possible peer leader cohorts represent the characteristics of the larger student body with the exception of the academic performance. As already suggested, we believe peer leaders should have academic credentials and accomplishments that exceed the norms of the rest of the student body.

9.   We recommend that campuses not currently providing peer leader training through some kind of formal credit-bearing course, consider doing so. The course should provide specific instruction on the peer leader's duties and the rationale supporting them. The course should also provide a body of knowledge immediately applicable to the role of peer leader, such as interpersonal communication and group process skills, leadership styles, learning styles, student development theory, etc.

10. There is a tremendous shortage of assessment on the effectiveness of peer leader programs, especially of assessment that moves beyond levels of student satisfaction. We need to know more about the impact of such programs on both the peer leaders and the students they serve. For example, does participation in a peer leader program make any measurable difference on vocational selection and/or levels of community and civic engagement

of students after graduation? What is the impact on academic success and retention for both those who serve and those who are served? What are the potential cost savings to institutions for incorporating peer leaders into academic and administrative service functions? What impact does this have on the quality of service provided to students at the institution?

11. In the last decade, the national surveys of first-year seminar programs conducted by the University of South Carolina's National Resource Center for The First-Year Experience and Students in Transition have found that fewer than 10% of first-year seminars include peer instruction (Barefoot & Fidler, 1992; Barefoot & Fidler, 1996; Barefoot, 1998; Warnock, 2001). Although some increase has occurred, future research needs to focus on why this component has not attracted more interest.

12. In spite of the excellent program examples from community colleges in this volume, these institutions are underrepresented, particularly in the use of peer leaders in first-year seminar courses. Because of the open door admissions role of community colleges and the potential for greater numbers of "at risk" students, peer leader programs may be even more critical in these settings—especially as public policy directs increasingly larger and larger numbers of first-time college students into the two-year public sector. Higher educators in the two-year sector need to lobby for increased attention to the potential benefits of peer leadership.

13. Of course, there is much we still do not know about the impact of the technological revolution on learning and satisfaction in college students. We do know that this revolution is transforming teaching and other communication environments on our campuses. We recommend that program coordinators begin to study the interactions between peer instruction and technology on their campuses.

14. Is the work of peer leaders being adequately recognized and affirmed through membership in elite academic honor societies on our campuses? Does consideration need to be given to the establishment of some type of national student honor society exclusively for recognition of peer leaders?

15. There is much that we do not know about how the use of peers in the educational process may change the nature of teaching and learning, for better or worse. We need to study the impact of peers on teaching and learning. We also need to know more about how the use of peer leaders impacts the roles of academic administrators, student affairs professionals, and faculty.

In this conclusion, we have highlighted a number of areas for investigation in the field of peer leadership. We are optimistic about the future of peer leaders and peer leadership programs on our campuses. We hope this publication will help institutions as they engage in conversations on how to serve students by optimizing the talents of outstanding paraprofessionals. Further, we hope the ideas raised here will serve as a preliminary conceptual framework for further studies on peer leadership and its impact on college students and institutions of higher education.

References

Barefoot, B. O. (1998). *1997 national survey of first-year seminar programs*. Unpublished summary. Retrieved on March 5, 2001 from the World Wide Web: www.sc.edu/fye/resources/surveys/survey97.htm.

Barefoot, B. O., & Fidler, P. P. (1992). *The 1991 national survey of freshman seminar programming* (Monograph No. 10). Columbia, SC: University of South Carolina, National Resource Center for The Freshman Year Experience.

Barefoot, B. O., & Fidler, P. P. (1996). *The 1994 national survey of freshman seminar programs* (Monograph No. 20). Columbia, SC: University of South Carolina, National Resource Center for The Freshman Year Experience and Students in Transition.

Warnock, C. (2001). *2000 national survey of first-year seminar programs*. Unpublished summary. Available: National Resource Center for The First-Year Experience and Students in Transition, University of South Carolina, Columbia, SC 29208.

RECRUITMENT, SELECTION, AND TRAINING

UNIVERSITY OF SOUTH CAROLINA

2001 Peer Leader
Recruitment and Selection Time Line

Date	Task/Event
September 5	Request faculty/administration and student organization mailing materials, get labels from Registrar's Office for students who currently have at least a 3.0 GPA or higher
September 18 – 22	Send recruitment letter with nomination form to current peer leaders, graduate leaders, U101 faculty, faculty and administrators
September 26 – 27	Recruit PL's assistance for organization presentations/flyer distribution on 9/29 (create list of buildings sign-up sheet)
September 29	Post Flyer/Posters with brochures around campus (Selected buildings: Wardlaw, BA, Honors College, RHUU, Preston) and in residence halls, Greek housing
	Applications completed and sent to printer
October 9, 11, 13	*Gamecock* Brief about nominations for PL's
October 18	Reminder letter about nominations
October 11 – November 10	Presentations to selected organization meetings *(Fall Break October 16 – 17)
October 27	Nomination preferred submission date
October 30	Begin to send out thank you letter to nominators
November 6 – 17	Ad on RHA Channel
November 6 – 30	Call those on the nomination lists about applying
November 13, 15	Article in the *Gamecock*
November 20, 27	Gamecock Brief about application deadline

November 30	Suggested deadline for applications; begin rolling review of applications
January 17	*Gamecock* brief reminder of last deadline for PL
January 22	Final application deadline
January 24 & 25	Hold interviews for borderline candidates
January 26	Final notification of selection
January 31 & February 7 February 1, 8	Training Workshops
March 22	Mandatory reception to meet instructors (PL, GL and instructors) *tentative
April 5, 9	Team-Building Mini-Workshops

Paving the Way...

UNIVERSITY 101 PEER LEADER APPLICATION FORM

PREFERRED SUBMISSION DATE: **Thursday, November 30, 2000**
DEADLINE: **Monday, January 22, 2001**

Please return application to the University 101 Office at 1629 Pendleton St.

Questions? Contact Jennifer Clark @ 777-3801 or Rebecca Lerch @ 777-1941

Name _____ Social Security # _____

Local Address _____ Phone _____

Permanent Address _____ Phone _____

E-mail Address _____

Academic Status for 2001-02 school year: Senior _____   Junior _____

Cumulative GPA _____   Did you transfer to USC? _____

What is your College? _____   Major? _____

I acknowledge that the information in this application is factual and is a realistic assessment of my abilities. Because I recognize that being a University 101 Peer Leader carries with it both privileges and responsibilities, I hereby give permission to the University 101 Office to obtain information from the Office of Student Discipline regarding any disciplinary records in my name. This information will be used for the sole purpose of determining my personal attributes and suitability for this position.

_____   _____
Signature   Date

Please include a Verification Form stating your earned credit hours and
GPA from the Registrar's Office.

The University 101 Program, within the University of South Carolina, provides affirmative action and equal opportunity in education and employment for all qualified persons regardless of race, color, religion, sex, national origin, age, disability, or veteran status.

(Continued ⇒)

Please answer the following questions (feel free to use additional pages if necessary):

1. Please list your major campus and community involvements. Include any awards you have received, and any positions you have held.

2. Please list all relevant work experiences (including internships, work study, part-time or summer job, etc.).

3. What are your career goals/plans?

4. Define what it means to be a University 101 Peer Leader. Describe what you perceive to be the role of a Peer leader and how you would perform such a role if you are selected.

5. Describe in detail your personal qualifications that would contribute to the success of first-year students and to the University 101 Peer Leaders Program.

FAIRFIELD UNIVERSITY
Junior Year of Service
Application for 1999 Leadership Positions

All students wishing to be a FYE Facilitator for the Fall 1999 should use this application whether they will be a junior next year or not. Freshmen should give an estimated GPA.

PERSONAL INFORMATION

Name _____ Major _____

Year _____ Semester GPA _____ Cumulative GPA _____

Date of Birth _____ Social Security Number _____

HOME INFORMATION

Street Address _____

City, State, Zip _____

Phone Number _____

SCHOOL INFORMATION

Box Number _____

Residence Hall (if not a commuter) _____

Phone Number _____

APPLICATION INFORMATION:

References

Please list three people (2 from Fairfield University) who have known you for more than one year who are qualified to comment on your ability to hold the position for which you are applying.

1. Name: _____ Phone: _____

2. Name: _____ Phone: _____

3. Name: _____ Phone: _____

Application Deadlines:

All applications should be returned to the Barone Campus Center Main Office.

New Student Programs

Coordinator Positions   Friday, November 13, 1998
First Year Experience Facilitator   Wednesday, December 9, 1998
Orientation Committee Members   Wednesday, February 10, 1999

Senior Week

Students interested in applying for a Senior Week 2000 position should indicate their interest on the Junior Year of Service brochure response card. Applications will be sent in October 1999 for a November 1999 selection.

Please check the positions you would like to be considered for. You may check more than one.

NEW STUDENT PROGRAMS
❑ Executive Coordinator
❑ First Year Experience Coordinator
Coordinator Positions:
❑ Parent Programs
❑ Special Events
❑ Student Entertainment
❑ Administrative Needs
❑ Special Programs
❑ Academics & Opening
❑ External Relations
❑ Arrival and Traffic
Other:
❑ First Year Experience Facilitator
❑ Committee Member
   Committee Name:
   _____

SENIOR WEEK
❑ Senior Week Co-Chairs
Sub-Chair Positions:
❑ Jesuit Social
❑ Pub Night
❑ Senior Picnic
❑ Semiformal
❑ Parents Dance
❑ Bon Fire
❑ Senior Slide Show
❑ Administrative Assistant
❑ Tickets
❑ Cruise
❑ Parents Needs
❑ Workers Needs
❑ Security
Other:
❑ Committee Member
   Committee Name:
   _____

(Continued ⇒)

Interviews

Students applying for one of the New Student Programs Coordinator positions should indicate what days of the week and times would be best for a 20 minute interview. All others will be contacted with interview information.

Days of the Week   *Times*

1. _____

2. _____

3. _____

QUESTIONS

Please answer the following questions to the best of your ability. Please feel free to attached additional sheets as needed. Answers for each questions should be a maximum of 3 type written paragraphs.

1. List activities that you have been involved in while at Fairfield University (i.e. community service, clubs & organizations, student employment, etc.)

ACTIVITY   POSITION   DATES OF INVOLVEMENT

_____

_____

2. Why are you interested in the position(s) that you are applying for?

3. Describe the role that you are applying for as you perceive it and how will you balance your time commitment.

4. What contributions do you see yourself making to the program?

As an applicant for one of the leadership positions contained on the front of this application, I hereby claim the information contained in this application is correct to the best of my knowledge. I understand that in the case of orientation, I am being selected into this advanced leadership position as an academic and social role model for new students. As such, I authorize the Office of New Student Programs to check both my academic and judicial records to determine my eligibility for the position for which I am applying. If accepted as a FYE facilitator, I understand that violating Fairfield University policies, especially those dealing with alcohol, can result in my forfeiting of my duties assigned to me as a FYE Facilitator.

Applicant Signature _____   Date _____

Questions

New Student Programs contact: Senior Week contact:
Timothy P. Lloyd   Matthew Dinnan
Director of New Student Programs   Director of the Barone Campus Center
Phone #: 254-4000, ext. 2375   Phone #: 254-4000, ext. 2371
E-mail: tlloyd@fairl.fairfield.edu   E-mail: madinnan@fairl.fairfield.edu

Return the completed application to the Barone Campus Center Main Office.

DELAWARE TECHNICAL AND COMMUNITY COLLEGE
Peer Associate Application

Name: _____   SS#: _____

Address: _____

City / State: _____   Zip Code: _____

Phone: _____   Class Year: ☐ 1st Year   ☐ 2nd Year

Academic Major: _____

Current GPA: _____   Applied For Financial Aid: ☐ Yes ☐ No

List and describe any extracurricular activities and/or jobs you plan to hold in the upcoming year:

ESSAY QUESTIONS:

1. Why are you interested in becoming a Peer Associate? What do you hope to learn?

2. What are own career plans (to date)?

3. Name two skills you possess that would make you a good Peer Associate. Illustrate these skills by using your work experience and/or extracurricular activities as examples.

4. How would your friends describe you? What characteristics and values would they attribute to you?

5. Briefly describe an incident in your college experiences in which you feel you helped an individual or group resolve a dilemma/conflict.

Recommendations: Please attach three (3) faculty and/or staff recommendations to this application.

Special Note for Financial Aid Recipients or Potential Financial Aid Recipients: If a student is eligible for the Federal College Work Study Program for any amount greater than the $300.00 work-ship scholarship, then the $300.00 work-ship scholarship will be void. If a student has been selected for the Peer Associate Program and is also eligible for the Federal College Work Study Program payment for hours of service will be made from the Federal College Work Study Program and not from the work-ship scholarship. If this condition applies to you, please read all conditions stipulated in the Federal College Work Study Program.

Any student eligible for financial aid may have his or her financial aid award reduced by the value of the work-ship scholarship. Please contact the Financial Aid Office for more information.

DELAWARE TECHNICAL AND COMMUNITY COLLEGE
Faculty or Administrator Recommendation

For Peer Associate Candidate

Candidate's Name: _____

I ☐ waive ☐ do not waive the right to review the contents of this recommendation I understand that signing this waiver statement is optional.

_____   _____
Candidate's Signature   Date

The above named candidate has applied for the position of Peer Associate, a position which requires maturity, dependability, and an evident enthusiasm for serving students and the College.

Please complete this section by circling the response that best reflects your judgement of the candidate in that area.

1= always, 2 = almost always, 3 = sometimes, 4 = seldom, 5 = never, NA = not able to judge the candidate:

1. works well independently	1	2	3	4	5	NA
2. works well in groups	1	2	3	4	5	NA
3. is mature	1	2	3	4	5	NA
4. is effective in stressful situations	1	2	3	4	5	NA
5. demonstrates leadership qualities	1	2	3	4	5	NA
6. is tolerant of others	1	2	3	4	5	NA
7. has developed good listening skills	1	2	3	4	5	NA
8. is flexible	1	2	3	4	5	NA
9. is approachable	1	2	3	4	5	NA
10. is perceptive	1	2	3	4	5	NA
11. is honest and trustworthy	1	2	3	4	5	NA
12. is cooperative, reliable, and dependable	1	2	3	4	5	NA
13. communicates well with students	1	2	3	4	5	NA

DELAWARE TECHNICAL AND COMMUNITY COLLEGE
Peer Associate Rating Form

Applicant: _____   Technology: _____

Position: Peer Associate-Wilmington Campus   Date: _____

Section 1 – Interview Rating

Use the following scale to rate the applicant during the interview
5: Exceptional   2: Below Average   3: Average
4: Above Average-Strong 1: Unacceptable   0: Unobserved

_____ Desire as a Helper	_____ Learning Ability
_____ Experience	_____ Verbal Communication
_____ Attention to Detail	_____ Stress Tolerance
_____ Cooperation	_____ Problem Solving
_____ Initiative	_____ Knowledge About DTCC
_____ Interpersonal Skills	

Total Points: _____ (out of 55 possible points)

Section 2 – Overall Interview Rating:

_____ Exceptional (5)	_____ Strong (4)	_____ Acceptable (3)
_____ Average (2)	_____ Weak (1)	_____ Unacceptable (0)

Section 3 – Recommendations:

1: _____ (out of 10 points)   # 2: _____ (out of 10 points)

3: _____ (out of 10 points)

Section 4 – Student Essays: _____ (out of 50 points - 10 points per question)

Section 5 – GPA: _____ (10 points if at minimum or better)

Section 6 – Interviewer General Impression: _____ (out of 10 total possible points)

Total Candidate Points: _____ (out of 160 total possible points)

Interviewer Name (PRINT): _____

Interviewer Signature: _____

LEE UNIVERSITY
Application for Peer Leaders
Fall 2000

Personal Information

Name _____ Major _____

Date of Birth _____ Social Security Number _____

Classification _____ Cumulative GPA _____

I give permission for the First-Year Experience Peer Leadership Committee to check my GPA.

Signature _____

Home/Summer Information

Street Address _____

City, State, Zip _____

Phone Number _____

School Information

Box Number _____

Present Phone Number _____

References (one must be a member of the Lee University faculty):

1. Name: _____ Phone: _____

2. Name: _____ Phone: _____

3. Name: _____ Phone: _____

Please attach a separate page for each of the following:

I. List your activities and involvements while at Lee (please include your duration of participation and any leadership positions held).

II. Tell us about your GST101 Experience. Be sure to include the name of the instructor and the semester in which the course was taken. (All responses will be kept confidential).

> Please return all applications to Suzanne Hamid, Director of First-Year Programs, Vest Building 101. **Deadline for submission is Friday, April 7.** Please hand deliver your applications to my office. When you get there, sign-up sheets for interview times will be posted on the door. Please sign up for a time most convenient for you. **Interviews will be conducted between April 10 – 13.** Fall 2000 Peer Leaders will be selected by Thursday, April 18. Please direct further questions to Ms. Hamid at 614-8623.

♦ If selected as a Peer Leader, I will commit to fulfill all of the responsibilities associated with this position.

Signature _____

♦ If selected as a Peer Leader, I will uphold the standards of the Lee University Community Covenant.

Signature _____

DELAWARE TECHNICAL AND COMMUNITY COLLEGE
Peer Associate Agreement

I, _____ accept all of the responsibilities and duties which come with my participation in the Peer Associate Program on the _____ Campus of Delaware Technical & Community College. I understand that I will be awarded a bookstore scholarship for these duties based on a "work-ship" (working scholarship) premise. I agree to perform these duties for a $300.00 bookstore scholarship at the _____ Campus Bookstore. I understand that I may charge my books and supplies up to $300.00 at the start of an academic term. If payment for books and supplies has already been made, I may then use the $300.00 to pay for any outstanding tuition and fee payments to the College. If any funds remain the balance of payment will be made at the end of the designated semester in the form of an expense check. For this $300.00 work-ship scholarship, I agree to perform 60 hours of service during the _____ semester of the _____ year. My training will be conducted and monitored by the Peer Associate Program Supervisor.

I understand that I may reapply for this work-ship scholarship but I am not guaranteed a peer associate position in future terms. To be reconsidered for this position I must maintain at least a 3.0 G.P.A. and submit a letter requesting reconsideration prior to the next academic term.

I understand that my work-ship scholarship can be terminated at any time should I fail to conduct myself in an appropriate manner. My position may also be terminated should I fail to fulfill the required hours of training and service.

I further understand I must maintain my academic standing as an enrolled Delaware Tech student during the term of this agreement. Any official or unofficial withdrawal from the college will void this agreement.

Penalty for failing to complete all required aspects of this contract will be to refund any charges credited to my bookstore account and forfeit any unused portion of the work-ship scholarship to the college.

Note: Any student eligible for financial aid may have his or her financial aid award reduced by the value of their work-ship scholarship. Please contact the Financial Aid Office for more information.

This contract is from _____ to _____ for semester(s) _____ and/or _____
I agree to all terms specified in this agreement.

_____
Student Name (Print)

_____
Social Security #

_____
Student Signature

_____
Date

_____
Dean of Student Services

_____
Date

_____
Peer Associate Program Supervisor Signature

_____
Date

KEAN UNIVERSITY
Peer Liaison Contract

The purpose of this contract is to state the responsibilities of the Peer Liaison. After carefully reading the contract, both the Peer Liaison and Peer Liaison Coordinator will sign it, and a copy will be kept in your file at CNS.

1. I will attend the following *mandatory* events: Peer Liaison Training Programs (Spring and Summer), Instructor /Peer Training (May), Registration Training (May), Monthly Team Meetings, New Student Orientation, Celebration of Diversity Workshops (with F. S. class), and Career 2000 (with F. S. class).

2. In addition to the above, I will attend <u>two</u> of the following orientation programs:
   _____ Adult Student Orientation Program (September)
   _____ Transfer Orientation Program (June)
   _____ Transfer Orientation Program (August)
   _____ Family Orientation Program (September)

3. As a Peer Liaison, I am responsible to attend a minimum of <u>two</u> freshman registration periods in either June, July, or August to assist the newly admitted freshmen with academic advisement.

4. I will also sign-up to assist the CNS staff at various programs throughout the year.

5. I understand my responsibility regarding academic integrity. Plagiarism, cheating, and other forms of academic dishonesty may result in disciplinary action which could include dismissal from the University.

6. I will call and speak to the Peer Liaison Coordinator, secretaries, or other staff members if I am going to be late or absent.

7. Absences, lateness, or early departures must be kept to a minimum in order to meet my job responsibilities and remain a Peer Liaison.

8. Peer Liaisons working evening hours are responsible for finding a replacement if they are going to be absent or late.

9. I understand that I must maintain a minimum cumulative grade point average of 2.5 in order to remain a Peer Liaison. Therefore, I give permission to the Peer Liaison Coordinator to periodically check my academic file to verify my grade point average. All information will be kept confidential.

10. I will fulfill all of the responsibilities delegated to me by the instructor of my Freshman Seminar class including preparing for the class, scheduling an appointment time with each student, and attending all of the F. S. classes.

11. I will be kind, considerate, and respectful to my Freshman Seminar instructor, students, and fellow workers.

12. I will perform the CNS responsibilities delegated to me by the staff with a positive attitude.

13. I will clarify instructions and communications from the staff of the Center for New Students in order to perform tasks to the best of my ability.

14. I will participate in two fundraisers (one each semester) for the Peer Liaison Club.

15. Since I am employed in the Center for New Students, I am not able to work in another University department.

16. I understand that my salary will be no more or no less than $6.25 per hour. New Team Leaders will make $6.50 per hour. Experienced Team Leaders will make $7.00 per hour. I must work a minimum of 4 hours, maximum of 10 hours per week. Team Leaders must work a minimum of 10 hours, maximum of 15 hours per week.

17. I am aware that there will be a mid-term and end of the semester evaluation of my performance as a Peer Liaison and Center for New Students worker.

18. I understand that if I am not fulfilling my job responsibilities or contract requirements my position of Peer Liaison will be terminated.

19. I understand it is my responsibility to assist with the cleaning and upkeep of the office.

Signature of Applicant   _____

Coordinator's Signature   _____

Center for New Students
Kean University
Union, NJ 07083

LEE UNIVERSITY
Office Of First Year Programs

The President and the Office of First Year Programs of Lee University, submit this contract for your acceptance.

Your compensation is fixed and shall be paid according to the agreement for teaching Gateway to University Success.

I agree to discharge such duties as may be assigned to my position as detailed below:

I. **SYLLABUS**
   A. I agree to implement the syllabus as agreed upon and prepared by the Office of First Year Programs.
   B. I agree to abide by the evaluation activities as prescribed by the above said syllabus and which include the following

1.	Attendance/Participation in class	5%
2.	Quizzes	20%
3.	Introduction to autobiography	5%
4.	Chapters 1 – 4 of autobiography	40% (10% per chapter)
5.	Advisor interview	10%
6.	Conclusion of autobiography	10%
7.	Service project	5%
8.	Attendance on final exam day	5%

II. **COURSE CONTENT**
   A. I agree to use the text and instructor's manual in the teaching and planning of the course.
   B. I agree to use the resource manual and the 30-Day Planner in the teaching and planning of the course.

III. **ADDITIONAL TASKS**
   A. I agree to attend the two-day Gateway to University Success retreat prior to commencing the fall semester.
   B. I agree to meet with my class and participate in New Student Orientation.
   C. I agree to facilitate an out-of-class activity for my Gateway to University Success class (e.g., a meal at the professor's home).
   D. At the end of the semester and at the end of the following semester, I agree to contact my Gateway to University Success students who indicate that they will not continue active student enrollment.
   E. Further I agree to record and report the students' response.

IV. **PROFESSIONAL RELATIONSHIP EXPECTATIONS**
   A. I agree to meet weekly for planning sessions with my peer leader.
   B. I agree to work in harmony with my team leader and attend team meetings as called by my respective team leader.

C. I agree to cooperate with the team leader in planning three to five joint sessions for your team. Attendance is expected at the planning sessions and the actual events.
D. I agree to maintain active contact with the office of the Director of First Year Programs.
E. I agree to maintain timeliness in all correspondence with the Director of First Year Programs (e.g., voice mail, e-mail, and memoranda).

Acceptance
I hereby accept this and agree to abide by the above conditions and expectations.

Date: _____ Signed: _____

UNIVERSITY OF SOUTH CAROLINA
EDLP 520 – The Teacher as Manager
Fall 2000
Section 2, Wednesdays — 5:00-6:15 p.m.

Stuart Hunter
Director, National Resource Center
for The First-Year Experience and
Students in Transition
1728 College Street
Work: 777-4761
E-mail: stuarth@gwm.sc.edu

Jennifer Clark
Graduate Assistant, University 101
1629 Pendleton Street
Work: 777-3801
E-mail: clarkjn@gwm.sc.edu

EDLP 520 & Prerequisites

These special sections of EDLP 520 are restricted to those students serving as Peer Leaders for University 101 classes during the semester in which they enroll in EDLP 520. Prerequisites to enrollment in these sections include completion of the Peer Leader Training Workshops (6 contact hours) held in February 2000 and participation in a team building session with your University 101 instructor/team teacher (12 contact hours) held Spring 2000.

EDLP 520 is a unique class which is designed to provide a forum for the evaluation, reflection, and processing of your experiences as a Peer Leader in University 101. The discussion will revolve around such topics as teaching techniques, classroom management strategies, student development theories, lesson plan development, and other related issues. It might be useful for you to consider the approximately 40 contact hours in University 101 as a lab or practicum, with the additional 9 class meetings of the EDLP 520 class as a discussion/lecture class.

Attendance Policy

Benefits of this class can only be gained when **ALL** members are present to contribute to discussions. Therefore, attendance is expected at all class times. In extreme situations when it is impossible for you to attend, you are responsible for contacting one of the instructors BEFORE class.

Expectation of Academic Honesty and Confidentiality

The culture we will create in this class is one of openness, sharing, and learning from one another. The comments shared in the discussions should be considered confidential and should not be repeated outside the class. Because this course focuses on your personal and individual experience, it is expected that all work submitted will be yours and yours alone. Any work presented that is not your own will be considered a violation of the *Carolinian Creed* and will not receive credit.

Assignments

1. *Journal* – Each student will be responsible for maintaining a journal throughout the semester to record experiences, thoughts, and insights from the University 101 class. The journal should include reflections on your experiences in your University 101 classes, your teamwork with your professor, and your observations on the students in the University 101 class. This journal will be turned in at the mid-point of the semester and will be reviewed near the end of the semester. The journal can be handwritten or typed.
2. A peer leader *listserv* has been established for the sharing of good ideas, successful experiences, and solicitation of assistance from fellow peer leaders throughout the semester. Participation is expected. Please see attached instructions.
3. *Midterm Exam* – The take-home essay midterm exam will take the form of a guided reflection on your role as a peer leader, your perceptions of the students in your class, your relationship with your instructor, and your growth and development as a student. It must be typed and double-spaced.
4. *Model Lesson/Class* – Each student will be responsible for developing an original model University 101 lesson plan. Resources will be provided to assist with the development of this model class outline. It must be typed and double-spaced.
5. *Final Assessment* – This final paper should explore your most significant contributions and experiences related to the responsibilities of a University 101 Peer Leader. Specific sections of the paper will be explained in detail further into the course. It must be typed and double-spaced.
6. *Individual Conference* – An individual meeting is required with either instructor and should be scheduled individually, no later than mid-term.

Textbooks

1. *Peer Leader Tool Kit.* Will be distributed in class. Each student should become familiar with handouts found in the Tool Kit for it will provide many resources for co-teaching.
2. Textbooks for University 101. These textbooks may vary depending on your University 101 section. Some may be: *Your College Experience, Becoming a Master Student, The Norton Reader,* etc.
3. *Transitions 2000.* The University 101 Student Handbook
4. *Teaching at USC.* Will be distributed in class.
5. *Students Helping Students: A Guide for Peer Educators on College Campuses,* Ender & Newton, Jossey-Bass. Will be distributed in class.

Final Grades

The final grade will be determined as follows:

1. Evaluation of the required written assignments
2. Participation in EDLP 520 and on the peer leader listserv
3. Assessment by University 101 instructor with whom the peer leader taught

Final Exam – Wednesday, December 13, 5:30 p.m.

EDLP 520
Course Outline

DATE	CLASS TOPIC	ASSIGNMENTS DUE
August 23	"KICK-OFF" LUNCHEON/ORIENTATION IN RH 203	
August 30	Getting Reacquainted	
September 13	Syllabus Critique Review of Four Phases of U101	u Subscribe/post message to Listserv u Read: *Teaching at USC* pg. 7-8, 9-10, 15-16 u One-page paper on syllabus
September 27	Model Lesson Plan Intro & Discussion Team Teaching & Communication Begin Mid-semester Conference	u Read *Teaching at USC* pg. 51-57 and *SHS* pg. 168-177, 177-186
October 11	Student Development Theory Presentation of Model Lesson Plans Midterms Distributed	u Read: *SHS*, Chapter 2 u Bring copies of Model Lesson Plans
October 25	Finish Model Lesson Assessment in U101 Classes Your Needs Assessment	u Midterm due u Journal turned in for review u Conferences completed
November 8	Individual Student Needs & Characteristics and Student Sub-populations Study Abroad Presentation	u Read: *Teaching at USC*, pg. 58-68; *SHS*, pg. 52-56, 61-65; Zuker's *Stress Points in the College Transition*
November 15	TBA	
November 29	TBA Final Exam Distributed	
December 6	Final Class Social	u Optional Final Due Date u Submit Journal
December 13	Final Exam Due by 5:30 p.m. to Stuart at 1728 College Street	

UNIVERSITY OF MARYLAND, COLLEGE PARK
EDUC 388/EDC1 498
Guided Experiences in College Teaching

Dr. Gerry Strumpf
Director of Orientation
Orientation Office
0221 Stamp Student Union
(301) 314-8213 (work)
gstrumpf@umdacc.umd.edu

Matthew Wawrzynski
Assistant to the Director
Orientation Office
0229 Stamp Student Union
(301) 314-8214 (work)
mwawrzyn@deans.umd.edu

Office hours by appointment. Students are encouraged to make appointments to discuss any aspects of the course or the UTA program.

UTA Responsibilities:

1. 8 - 10 hours per week of teaching assistantship as determined by you and your mentor

2. Full participation in UTA seminars and completion of assignments.

Purposes of the Seminar:
♦ to increase an understanding of the first-year student experience
♦ to explore effective methods of college teaching
♦ to provide opportunities and methods for reflection
♦ to integrate seminar discussions on diversity, ethics, social justice, community, and civic responsibility with classroom experiences
♦ to increase students' ability to work in groups
♦ to develop a spirit of reflection, inquiry, and critical thinking about developmental issues
♦ to explore together, challenge ourselves, and learn from one another

Grades: Grades are determined by averaging a grade for the teaching assistant responsibilities (grade assigned by your faculty instructor or co-teaching assistant) and a grade assigned for the seminar portion. In addition, a brief evaluative description of your work will be requested from your faculty instructor or co-teaching assistant.

Assignments:

Attendance/promptness (more than 2 absences = 1 letter grade drop)

   Note: Due to the nature of the seminar, attendance is of primary importance.

Significance of participation

Maintenance/currency/quality of the UTA journal

Performance of individual class assignments/readings

Completion of final analytical assessment of teaching paper

There are no tests or formal examinations.

There will be readings each week; those readings not in the reading packet will be distributed in class.

Both in compliance with and in the spirit of the Americans with Disabilities Act (ADA), we would like to work with you if you have a disability that is relevant to your coursework and requires academic accommodations. Please contact the instructors as soon as possible.

Notes on the UTA Journal:

The UTA Journal is the major ongoing assignment for the seminar portion of your experience. It is intended to be a vehicle for reflection on your experience and an opportunity to crystallize and verbalize your analysis of, and feelings about that experience. It is not a handbook of ideas gathered in seminar sessions; and it is not a diary!

You are required to send electronic journal submissions each week to Matt for comments and feedback. In this way, you can be assured of some personal dialogue throughout the semester (over and above the seminar sessions) and some regular feedback on your reflections. In addition, you should submit plans, quizzes, articles, audiovisual aid creations or other items which you create to assist your own or your mentor's teaching. These items can become part of your portfolio for your final assessment.

Appropriate Items for the Journal:

1. Discussion of your work as a teaching assistant
2. Discussion of seminar presentations, discussions, readings, etc.
3. Discussion of your UTA experience in relation to your own education, both past and projected
4. Discussion of your UTA experience in relation to your future teaching or other work/study goals.
5. Other reflections and insights concerning the relevance of the UTA experience to any aspect of personal growth, usefulness to you now or later, or applications to issues and problems with which you are concerned.
6. "Portfolio" items to illustrate your activities and decisions.

In all cases, the emphasis should be on "critical" analysis and evaluation of your experience. Similarly, *you are expected to comment on all assigned readings* (text and/or handouts).

Classroom Discussion Guidelines:

Due to the content and the large amount of personal investment in the UTA experience, the classroom should be a supportive, developmental environment for everyone, and the guidelines should assist with this. An overview of the guidelines follows:
♦ Everyone will be given a chance to talk.
♦ When someone is speaking, everyone else should be listening.
♦ Differences in opinions are to be respected. We will not interrupt each other.
♦ Everyone should claim ownership for his/her own thoughts and feelings.
♦ We will acknowledge that racism, classism, sexism, heterosexism, and other institutionalized forms of oppression exist.

- We will acknowledge that one mechanism of institutionalized racism, classism, sexism, heterosexism, and the like is that we are all systematically misinformed about our own privileged and oppressed groups.
- We will agree not to blame others or ourselves for the misinformation we have learned, but to accept responsibility for not repeating misinformation after we have learned otherwise.
- We will assume that people-both the groups we study and the members of the class-always do the best they can.
- We will share information about our groups with other members of the class, and never demean, devalue, or in any way "put-down" people for their experiences.
- We will agree to combat actively the myths and stereotypes about our own groups and other groups so that we can break down the walls that prohibit group cooperation and group gain.
- We will work together to create a safe atmosphere for open discussion.

Texts and Readings:

Brookfield, S. (1990). *The skillful teacher.* San Francisco: Jossey-Bass.

Davis, B. (1993). *Tools for teaching.* San Francisco: Jossey-Bass.

Erickson, B. L., & Strommer, D. W. (1991). *Teaching college freshmen.* San Francisco: Jossey-Bass

Gruszewski, K. (1996, Fall). Advice to the class of 2000. *Indiana Alumni Mini Magazine,* 1-2.

Kirp, D. (1997). Those who can't: 27 ways of looking at a classroom. *Change, 11-18.*

London, H. (1996, November/December). How college affects first-generation students. *About Campus,* 9-13.

McIntosh, P. (1991). Unpacking the invisible knapsack. *Peace and Freedom.*

Rendón, L. (1998, March/April). Helping nontraditional students be successful in college. *About Campus,* 2-3.

Rendón, L. (1996, November/December). Life on the Border. *About Campus, 14-20.*

Swartzlander, S., Pace, D., & Stamler, V. (1993). The ethics of requiring students to write about their personal lives. *The Chronicle of Higher Education.*

Tinto, V. (1993). *Leaving college: Rethinking the causes and cures of student attrition.* Chicago: The University of Chicago Press

All students are expected to adhere to the Code of Academic Integrity. *All violations of the* Code *will be referred to the Student Honor Council.*

EDUC 388/EDC1 498
Weekly Outlook

Sept 1	**Who's Coming to College. First Year Student Retention Issues** The Scope and Patterning of Student Departure from Higher Education, Tinto, Ch.2; Upcraft & Gardner, Ch. 6; University of Maryland Statistics; The First Year Coping with Challenges and Changes, TCF, 24-45.
Sept 8	**Classroom Climate and Culture Considerations. Creating a positive classroom climate; the role of culture, gender, race, and other differences** Building Trust with Students, TST p. 163-176; Diversity and Complexity in the Classroom, TFT, p 39-51; Academic Accommodations for Students with Disabilities, TFT p 31-38;White Privilege: Unpacking the Invisible Knapsack, P&F, 10-12.
Sept 15	**Teaching Nuts and Bolts** Leading a Discussion, TFT, p 63-74; Some Truths about Skillful Teaching, TST, p 192-211; Encouraging Student Participation in Discussion, TFT, 75-81.
Sept 22	**Student Development Theory and Learning Styles** Learning Styles and Intellectual Development, TCF, p 46-62; Learning Styles and Preferences, TCF, p 185-192; Understanding the Tensions and Emotions of Learning, TST, 43-56.
Sept 29	**Helping Students Learn** Helping Students Learn, TCF, p 177-184; Developing Study and Learning Skills, TCF, p 198-216; Encouraging Student Involvement in the Classroom, TCF, 106-121.
Oct 6	**Discussions** Adjusting Teaching to the Rhythms of the Semester, TST, p 57-70; Preparing for Discussion, TST, p 88-101; Facilitating Discussions, TST, p 102-114; Strengthening Commitments to Freshman Teaching, TCF, 219-233.
Oct 13	**Myers-Briggs Type Indicator** Complete MBTI and bring to class; Intro to Type 5thEdition (booklet)
Oct 20	**Academic Advising** Advising and Mentoring as Teaching Opportunities, TCF, p 1T9-197.
Oct 27	No Class- Midterm Meetings with Matt *(turn in draft of first part of synthesis)*
Nov 3	**Critical Thinking** Knowing, Understanding, and Thinking, The Goals of Freshman Instruction, TCF, p 65-80.
Nov 10	**Motivating Students** Motivating Students, TFT, p 193-201.
Nov 17	**Diverse Populations** Helping Nontraditional Students be Successful in College, AC, p 2-3; Life on the Border, AC, 14-20; How College Affects First-Generation Students, AC, 9-13.
Nov 24	No Class - Work on final synthesis and portfolio
Dec 1	**Reflection and Assessment** The Ethics of Requiring Students to Write About Their Personal Lives, CHE; Those Who Can't 27 Ways of Looking at the Classroom, CHG, p 11-18; Advice to the Class of 2000, IU.
Dec 8	**Final Assessment** Final self-assessment papers due; evaluation of the UTA experience and seminar; portfolio discussions.

TCF = Teaching College Freshmen **TST** = The Skillful Teacher **CHG** = Change Magazine **CHE** = The Chronicle of Higher Education **TFT** = Tools for Teaching **AC** = About Campus **P&F** = Peace and Freedom **IU** = Indiana Alumni Magazine

DELAWARE TECHNICAL AND COMMUNITY COLLEGE
SSS 106 Becoming a Peer Helper - 1 Credit
Course Syllabus - Collegelink Program

Instructor: Louis C. Vangieri, M.S.
Counselor Delaware Technical & Community College
Student Development Center - Room 116 East Building
333 Shipley Street
Wilmington, DE 19801
(302) 571-5339 (Voice Mail)
E-Mail: lvangier@outland.dtcc.edu

Office Hours: By appointment.

Purpose. The purpose of this course is to build peer helping and leadership skills. Peer helping builds upon the natural helping skills and relationships which exist among students. Peer helpers and leaders can be trained to listen, share experiences, assist with decision-making, and provide support and practical assistance. Peer helpers have learned to cope with life challenges and are willing to help others in similar situations.

Course Methods. This course will not be a traditional college lecture course. Instead, there will be discussions, group work, reading, an ongoing journal, and lots of feedback from your instructor. The focus will be on active and collaborative learning, that is, learning by doing rather than by memorization.

Peer Associate Student Leaders. Delaware Tech Peer Associates are students who care about the well-being of their fellow classmates. Trained, informed Peer Associate Student Leaders give the phrase, "I know what you're going through," its true meaning. The Peer Associates will be part of the overall classroom experience.

Key Educational Issues to be Addressed:

♦ Student self-awareness skill development
♦ Non-verbal communication skill development
♦ Roadblocks to effective communication
♦ Developing listening skills
♦ Developing empathy skills
♦ Self-disclosure skill building
♦ Appropriate feedback and helping
♦ Decision-making and problem-solving skill development

Course Expectations:

♦ Attendance. The College attendance policy states: "Each student is expected to attend classes regularly in order to achieve maximum benefit from educational activities. Each student is responsible for all class work missed regardless of the reasons for absence." (Student Handbook) If you have to miss a class, please inform your instructor as soon as possible. Also, if you miss a class, you are responsible for getting class notes, handouts, etc. It is helpful to have telephone numbers of one or two classmates to get missed classroom information.

Remember: Excessive absences will impact your ability to earn points to successfully complete this course (specifically – your journals – journal assignments depend on your attendance in class; journal assignments cannot be made up if you miss a class).

◆ Freedom and Responsibility. In this class you are free to express your opinions and to share your ideas. With this freedom, however, comes the responsibility to do your best work, to turn in assignments on time, and to treat other class members with courtesy and respect.

◆ Academic Integrity. Please see the Policies and Procedures Section of your Student Handbook, specifically the College Policy for Student Responsibilities and Student Rights and the College Policy on Academic Dishonesty. All academic student work will be performed without resorting to cheating, plagiarism, lying and/or bribery. Severe penalties are possible for Violations. Please refer to your Student Handbook.

College Grading Policy: Final evaluations in any course are determined by the degree to which a student has met the measurable objectives of the course. Recorded grades include:

Grade	Grade Point	Numerical Value	Grade Interpretation
A	4.0	92 – 100	Measurable objectives were met in an outstanding manner
B	3.0	83 – 91	Measurable objectives were met in an above average manner
C	2.0	75 – 82	Measurable objectives were met
R	0.0	0 – 74	Measurable objectives were not met and the student must repeat the course – student attended course
U	0.0		Unofficial withdrawal (without College approval)— student stopped attending but did not drop course
I			Incomplete (temporary grade until student completes work)
WP			Withdrawal passing – assigned 4th to 8th week
WR			Withdrawal recycling – assigned 4th to 8th week

Grading for SSS 106 Becoming a Peer Helper. Grading for SSS 106 will be based on a point system and corresponds with the College grading policy to ensure students meet course objectives specified above.

920 points or better	A
830 – 919	B
750 – 829	C
Less than 750	R

1. *Session Journals* (660 points). You are required to submit a journal entry for each class session. Your instructor will provide you with a blank journal. Class attendance for completion of journals is required! Each journal is worth 60 points. You will be given an opportunity at the conclusion of each session to write in your journal. A late journal will have points reduced. Your journal will be graded based on the following criteria:

    ♦ All questions must be answered completely in line with course objectives.
    ♦ A comprehensive answer will blend class lecture information, information from the board, and your personal reactions to each question.

2. *In-Class Activities* (220 points). You must be present to earn points for these in-class activities. The in-class activity is worth 20 points for each activity. No points will be awarded to students who are not in attendance.

3. *Class Interview with Counselor* (100 points). One session will be devoted to interviewing a college counselor about his or her duties and about being an effective helper. Your instructor will provide you with a sample question list.

4. *Final Exam* (100 points). A comprehensive final essay examination will be given.

Class Texts:

Peer Counselor's Workbook by Gail Roberts. A student workbook which includes activities, poems, and peer leadership practical exercises.

Peer Associate Reference Manual compiled by Louis C. Vangieri, Counselor.

Class Outline:

5/17	Orientation - Syllabus Review, Class Expectations and Goals, Getting Acquainted
5/18	Non-Verbal Communications Skills (Session 2)
5/19	Roadblocks to Effective Communication (Session 3)
5/24	Listening and Empathy (Session 4)
5/25	Empathic Listening (Session 5)
5/26	Empathic Listening (Session 6)
6/1	Empathic Listening (Session 7)
6/2	Self- Disclosure (Session 8)
6/3	Feedback (Session 9)
6/7	Values Clarification (Session 10)
6/8	Decision Making and Problem Solving (Session 11)
6/9	Putting It All Together (Session 12)
6/10	Final Exam

PEER RESPONSIBILITIES/JOB DESCRIPTIONS

KEAN UNIVERSITY
Freshman Seminar
Peer Liaison Checklist Fall 1999

Things to be distributed/announced to your Freshman Seminar Class during the semester

Beginning of Semester

"X" or Date	TASKS	ACTION TO TAKE
	1. Orientation Evaluation Form	Collect after first class and bring to CNS
	2. Motivational Survey	Collect after first class and bring to CNS
	3. Contracts with Instructors	Bring to CNS by Thursday, September 9, 1999
	4. Orientation Packets	Distribute—early September
	5. Class Syllabus	Distribute; bring to CNS by Thursday, September 9, 1999
	6. Freshman Seminar Textbook	Tell how to get it/Distribute
	7. Turbo Account Form	Distribute
	8. Information Sheet (in textbook)	Have students complete; collect them for you files
	9. *Independent* (Kean newspaper)	Announce scoring for student collection project
	10. Events Calendar	Distribute
	11. Library Tour	Schedule with your class
	12. Computer Lab	Schedule with your class
	13. Voter Registration Forms	Distribute; collect; bring to CNS
	14. Appointments with individual students	Schedule by week of September 27

Middle of Semester

"X" or Date	TASKS	ACTION TO TAKE
	15. Career Service Center	Schedule visit
	16. Diversity Project	Announce; complete class project by October 28; collect; stamp co-curricular transcript
	17. Academic Integrity Booklet	Distribute
	18. Major Guide Sheet	Distribute
	19. Mid-semester Action Plan	Distribute during appointments
	20. Appointments with Individual Students	Schedule
	21. Registration Dates	Distribute; announce
	22. Co-curricular Transcript	Collect; stamp; bring to Freshman Seminar Director for Health Fair
	23. Spring, Fall, or Summer Bulletins	Distribute; announce

End of Semester

"X" or Date	TASKS	ACTION TO TAKE
	24. Background Knowledge Probe	Distribute; return to CNS by Thursday, December 9, 1999
	25. Student Evaluation Form	Distribute; collect; return to CNS by Thursday, December 9, 1999
	26. Peer Evaluation Form	Complete; return to CNS by Thursday, December 9, 1999
	27. Preliminary Summer Session List	Distribute (Spring Semester Only)

DELAWARE TECHNICAL AND COMMUNITY COLLEGE
Peer Associate Program
List of Potential Peer Associate Duties

1. Support counseling staff with group

2. Admission Orientation Sessions

3. College Planning Sessions

4. Write column for *Within Reach* Newsletter

5. Support counseling staff with counseling workshops (i.e., Stress Management, Balancing Work, School and Family, etc.)

6. Support training of student mentors in mentoring program

7. Assist students with completing admissions application

8. Assist students with career resources

9. Provide information and referrals for other campus services

10. Help coordinate logistics for special student services events

11. Talk with individual students

12. Keep accurate records of student contacts

13. Confer with counseling supervisor on a weekly basis

14. Periodically attend counseling staff meetings

15. Active involvement in Stanton/Wilmington Diversity Committee

16. Awareness of basic financial aid information

17. Work with multicultural students

ESTABLISHING PEER/INSTRUCTOR TEAMS

UNIVERSITY OF SOUTH CAROLINA
Agenda for Team-Building Workshops

I. **Welcome and Outline Format of Workshop** (15 minutes)

> **5:00-5:15 p.m.**

II. **Common Course Content** *(15 minutes)*

> **5:15-5:30 p.m.**

> *During this time we will review what is included in the Common Course Content. We will stress how much time each of these required components will take (this is especially helpful for syllabus planning). During the review, communication and syllabus planning will be stressed.*

III. **Team-Building Exercise to Form an Effective Partnership** *(30 minutes)*

> **5:30-6:00 p.m.**

> *Each teaching team will design strategies for teaching two or three of the requirements of the course at the same time. Teams may use the common course content handouts as guides. Each team will present their strategy to the group, and we will process it as a group.*

IV. **Roles and Responsibilities** *(30 minutes)*

> **6:00-6:30 p.m.**

> *Provide each teaching team with a handout outlining some roles and responsibilities that they may assume within their University 101 teaching teams. We should emphasize the following questions:*
> > *1. With respect to the handout, how would you as a team, divide/share these responsibilities?*
> > *2. What other areas of responsibility should be considered?*

V. **Closing Remarks**

UNIVERSITY OF SOUTH CAROLINA

Roles and Responsibilities Worksheet

Who will be responsible for the many facets of team-teaching University 101?

	Instructor	Graduate Student Leader	Peer Leader
Taking attendance/Communicating with students			
Corresponding with the students via e-mail/Maintaining a class listserv			
Grading, reading journals, and student papers			
Leading class discussion			
Making arrangements for guest speakers			
Providing information about campus events and student organizations			
Informing the students about the registration process			
Deciding what will appear on tests and quizzes			
Discussing *The Carolinian Creed* and personal responsibility issues			
Teaching various topics ranging from academic skills to health and wellness to financial management			
Organizing and scheduling community service activities			
Using *The State* newspaper			
Facilitation of computer/technological instruction			
Emphasizing notetaking and written and oral communication skills			

KEAN UNIVERSITY
Breaking the Ice
Between Peer and Instructor

1. What is the last movie you saw and liked?

2. What is the greatest lesson you've learned in your college experience?

3. What book most influenced your thinking?

4. What are your interests?   . . . hobbies?

5. Where do you want to be 10 years from now?

6. What keeps you at Kean?

KEAN UNIVERSITY
Peer Liaison Questionnaire

1. Why are you at this University? _____

   _____

2. Why do you want to be a Freshman Seminar Peer? _____

   _____

   _____

3. In a word or phrase describe your role (as you know it to be or as you believe it will be) in Freshman Seminar.

   A Peer Liaison is _____

4. In a word or phrase describe your relationship (as you know it to be or as you believe it will be) with your Instructor.

   My relationship with my Instructor is _____

5. How do you want your Instructor to treat you in class? _____

   _____

   _____

   _____

6. What are 5 things you want your Instructor to help you to do for the class?

   1. _____

   2. _____

   3. _____

   4. _____

   5. _____

7. What are 3 things you **do not** want your Instructor to do in the classroom?

   1. _____

   2. _____

3. _____

8. How will you be a learning team? _____

_____

_____

9. What are 3 things you will do to keep the lines of communication open with your Instructor throughout the semester?

1. _____

2. _____

3. _____

10. How will you work to resolve conflicts, should they arise, between you and your Instructor? _____

_____

_____

KEAN UNIVERSITY
Instructor Questionnaire

1. Why are you at this University? _____

   _____

2. Why do you want to be a Freshman Seminar Instructor? _____

   _____

   _____

3. In a word or phrase describe your role (as you know it to be or as you believe it will be) in Freshman Seminar

   An Instructor is_____

4. In a word describe your relationship (as you know it to be or as you believe it will be) with your Peer Liaison.

   My relationship with my Peer is _____

5. How do you want your Peer to treat you in class? _____

   _____

   _____

6. What are 5 things you want your Peer Liaison to do for the class?

   1. _____

   2. _____

   3. _____

   4. _____

   5. _____

7. What are 3 things you **do not** want your Peer Liaison to do in the classroom?

   1. _____

   2. _____

   3. _____

8.   How will you work to resolve conflicts, should they arise, between you and your Peer?

_____

_____

_____

9.   What are 3 things you will do to keep the lines of communication open with your Peer throughout the semester?

    1. _____

    2. _____

    3. _____

SAMPLE PEER/INSTRUCTOR CONTRACTS

KEAN UNIVERSITY
Freshman Seminar
Instructor-Peer Liaison Contracts
Guidelines

Each Freshman Seminar instructor and peer liaison will create a contract that spells out their roles in the Freshman Seminar. A jointly signed copy of this contract will be held by the instructor, the peer liaison, and the Center for New Students. The following guidelines can be used in preparation of the contract.

Professional Relationship Expectation

1. The Peer Liaison will:
   a. Maintain strict confidentiality about information shared between the peer liaison and students and with the instructor. (Any problematic or critical concerns expressed by students will be discussed with the instructor.)
   b. Dress and conduct him/herself in an exemplary manner, so as to be a role model for the students.
   c. Report to all class meetings and designated class/support group locations on time.
   d. Attend all scheduled planning/evaluation sessions with the instructor and participate actively with ideas and suggestions.
   e. Contact the instructor in advance by telephone, mail, or in person if unable to attend required meetings.

2. The Instructor will:
   a. Be supportive. Encourage the Peer Liaison in working with students and in carrying out specific tasks.
   b. Make suggestions for personal (attitudinal) improvement to promote interpersonal and leadership skills.
   c. Meet regularly with the Peer Liaison to plan and evaluate.
   d. Notify the Peer Liaison in person, by mail, or by telephone, in advance, of any changes in class meetings or special activities.

Task Expectations

1. The Peer Liaison will:
   a. Assist the Instructor with group activities such as tours, role plays, and discussions.
   b. Plan class activities as agreed by the Instructor and Peer Liaison.
   c. Set up a convenient time and place for small group interaction with students, if small groups are warranted, in the Freshman Seminar class.

    d. Be available to students at a designated time in the Center for New Students.

    e. Keep an information card on each student, including his/her birthday.

    f. Assist students with advance Summer/Fall/Spring Registration (i.e., course selection and form completion).

    g. On a weekly basis, share college activities that are pertinent to freshmen and other new students, and information from the Center for New Students.

    h. If requested by the Instructor, contact students who are absent, by telephone or mail, to ascertain reason(s) for absence, and help them catch up with class activities.

2. The Instructor will:

    a. Maintain attendance records, a personal data file and grades.

    b. Plan/coordinate all in and out of classroom activities/assignments, via syllabus.

    c. Conduct classes weekly.

    d. Design, administer, and score any tests.

    e. Evaluate all assignments given to students.

    f. Read and comment on all student logs.

_____   _____

Instructor's Signature   Peer Liaison's Signature

_____   _____

Date   Date

KEAN UNIVERSITY
Instructor/Peer Agreement

The following are expectations of the Instructor and Peer Liaison of the Freshman Seminar regarding relationships and task issues.

I. The Peer Liaison will:
   a. Maintain confidentiality regarding information shared between the Peer Liaison, students and instructor. Discuss problematic and critical concerns expressed by the students with the instructor;

   b. Always be a role model for the students in and out of the academic environment;

   c. Assist in presenting classroom activities; actively participate with ideas and suggestions; and attend all scheduled planning/evaluation sessions with the instructor;

   d. Contact the instructor if you are unable to attend required meetings or class;

   e. Be available to students at designated times in the Center for New Students;

   f. Assist students with advance registration;

   g. On a weekly basis, share college activities that are pertinent to freshman and information from the Center for New Students.

II. The Instructor will:

   a. Be supportive of and encouraging toward the Peer Liaison in working with students and in carrying out specific tasks;

   b. Meet regularly to plan and evaluate with Peer Liaison;

   c. Notify the Peer Liaison by telephone in advance regarding changes in scheduled meetings, activities, or class;

   d. Maintain a mentoring relationship with the Peer Liaison;

   e. Be professional at all times, in and out of the academic environment;

   f. Plan and coordinate classroom activities and assignments, via syllabus;

   g. Evaluate all assignments given to students.

Instructor:_____ Date:_____

Peer Liaison:_____ Date:_____

KEAN UNIVERSITY

Peer/Instructor Contract
(Form to be completed and submitted to the Freshman Seminar Director
by the first week of the semester.)

1. How will you refer to each other by name in/outside the classroom?

2. How will you physically position yourself within the classroom space when the other is teaching?

3. What are your classroom task expectations of each other? (example: 15 minutes of input, attendance, record keeper, etc.)?

4. What concrete input will the peer give in class?

5. How will you support each other in relation to the students? (Instructor should encourage students to meet with and not miss appointments with peer.)

6. What is your alternate plan if the instructor is absent?

7. When/Where will you meet each week to prepare for class?

8. How will you resolve conflicts with each other?

9. How will you provide feedback to each other to improve the class?

We agree to the mode of interacting as discussed above and will evaluate this contract at least once during the semester.

Peer _____ Date_____

Instructor _____ Date_____

PROGRAM EVALUATION

SOUTHWEST MISSOURI STATE UNIVERSITY
Peer Leader Evaluation by IDS Students

Peer Leader_____ Date_____

Please respond to the listed items by using the following rating scale:

4	Consistently Evident	Successfully demonstrates the skill at almost all appropriate opportunities
3	Frequently Evident	Acceptably demonstrates the skill but misses several opportunities to do so
2	Moderately Evident	Occasionally demonstrates the skill but misses numerous opportunities to do so
1	Slightly Evident	Infrequently and inconsistently demonstrates the skill
0	Not Evident	Does not demonstrate the skill

Rating <u>Personal and Individual skills</u>   <u>Comments</u>

_____ Demonstrates vitality, enthusiasm, and spontaneity
_____ Demonstrates confidence and a positive self-concept
_____ Is appropriately dressed and groomed
_____ Is friendly and understanding
_____ Is courteous, tactful, and patient
_____ Establishes appropriate relationships with students and teacher
_____ Upholds SMSU and IDS 110 policies/procedures
_____ Is dependable in attending IDS 110 class
_____ Is prompt (on time or early) in arriving to class
_____ Shows self-discipline, good judgment, and control (emotional & social)
_____ Works well with people from different ethnic/racial backgrounds

Rating <u>Instructional Support Skills</u>   <u>Comments</u>

_____ Positively reinforces teacher's instruction and activities
_____ Supports out-of-class activities (ex: conducting a tour)
_____ Is creative and displays initiative
_____ Participates in activities
_____ Helps call students who have been absent from class
_____ Uses correct English in speaking and writing
_____ Speaks clearly and distinctly with reasonable volume

Rating <u>Instructional Support Skills (cont.)</u>   <u>Comments</u>

    ____   Helps with classroom environment—chairs, chalkboard, etc.
    ____   Assists with videotape checkout, showing, and return
    ____   Presents a topic, activity, or exercise on occasion
    ____   Is knowledgeable about campus information and resources
    ____   Shares examples/experiences as a student at SMSU

Written Statements:

Please describe positive attributes, abilities, potential for growth, and areas to improve.

Explain the impact of the peer leader in your adjustment to SMSU and ability to excel in all your courses.

KEAN UNIVERSITY
Exit Interviews

Name:_____   Date:_____

1. Name two strengths you show as a Peer Liaison in the Center? Class?

2. Name two weaknesses you can identify as a Peer Liaison in the Center? Class?

3. What would be two contributions you will commit to make to the Center if hired back as a peer for fall 1999?

4. If you see the staff has implemented an office procedure that is not working, what are two courses of action you can take?

5. What are two examples of when you took initiative to complete tasks?

6. Since all of you are extremely busy, how do you plan to keep your schedules managed? Name two techniques.

7. Describe follow-up procedures when given a task. Give examples.

8. In your opinion, what are the two most important contributions you need to make to your Freshman Seminar class?

9. How would you help new peers adapt to working in the Center?

10. If faced with a crisis during the fall semester that affects your work as a peer, what would you do?

11. If you find yourself unhappy with your job in the Center (task not stimulating, overworked confused, etc.) what would you do?

12. If you are in need of advice because you have many questions concerning the Center but you are uncomfortable speaking with the Peer Coordinator name two other people you confide in (names/titles not necessary)?

13. Describe ways in which you can improve your attitude at work?

14. What are ways in which you limit yourself? In what ways can you address those limitations?

PEER LEADER PROGRAM QUESTIONNAIRE

LABEL GOES HERE

Please answer the following questions (handwritten or typed) and return no later than Friday, April 16. A stamped, addressed envelope is provided for your convenience.

---

1. General Information:

1. How old is your peer leader program? _____
2. Number of current peer leader. _____
3. Composition
   - Number of   Male _____   Female _____
   - Classifications: So _____   Jr _____   Sr _____
   - Semesters Served: 1 _____   2 _____   3 _____
4. Number of students served by current peer leaders. _____
5. Size of Institution: 0-3,000 _____ 3,000-10,000 _____
                                 10,000+ _____
6. Type of Institution: Public _____ Private _____

---

2. Rationale:
- Were you responsible for initiating/establishing your peer leader program?
  Yes _____ No _____
- If no, which department originally established your institution's peer leader program?

  _____

- If yes, briefly describe the reason(s) for wanting a peer leader program.

  _____

  _____

- List the major goals and objectives of your program. _____

  _____

  _____

- Which sector of your institution is responsible for your institution's peer leader Program? (Academic, Student Affairs, Other) _____

3. Administrative Challenges and Champions:
- Describe some of the biggest challenges in establishing, maintaining, and facilitating your peer leader program. _____

  _____

- Describe some of the biggest supports in establishing, maintaining, and facilitating the peer leader program (e.g., Key Personnel, Offices, Departments, etc.) _____

  _____

  _____

4. Selection Criteria:
- What criteria do you use in the selection of your peer leaders (G.P.A., Classification, Leadership Skills, etc.)? _____

_____

- What other items complete the application process (interview, personality test, letter of recommendation, essay, etc.)? _____

_____

- What are the methods used in recruitment (forms of advertising, notification, etc.)?

_____

- Have you been successful in attracting a sufficient number of applicants for your peer leader program? _____

- How are the peer leaders and instructors matched? _____

_____

- Who makes the final decision on the matching? _____

5. Training:
- Do you have a training program for your peer leaders? Yes _____ No _____
- If yes, please answer the following:
    - What is the format (course, seminar, retreat, etc.)? _____
    - Where does this training take place? _____
    - What is the length of the training session? _____
    - Who is responsible for organizing the event? _____
    - Who does the training? _____
    - Are the peer leaders and instructors trained together? Yes _____ No _____
    - Is the training a prerequisite for teaching the course? Yes _____ No _____
    - Please list some specific topics that are covered. _____

    _____

    - Are there any specific materials used such as a manual, textbook, etc.?

    _____

    - What is your estimated budget for this training? _____
    - Other: _____

6. Financial Commitments:
- How much money is allocated toward your peer leader program in the areas of:
    - Training: _____
    - Stipend: _____
    - Recruitment: _____
    - Other: _____

7. Duties and Responsibilities:
- What form of accountability do you use with the peer leaders (contract, policy and procedure manual, resource manual, etc.)? _____

_____

- Do you use peer leaders in any other course/area outside of the first-year seminar?
  Yes _____ No _____
- If yes, do you use the same peer leaders? Yes _____ No _____
- If yes, give examples of these courses/areas. _____
  _____

- Give examples of some specific duties performed by peer leaders in the first-year seminar class.
  _____
  _____

- How many hours are your Peer Leaders required to work? _____
- What percentage of the Freshman Seminar class are your Peer Leaders expected to teach?
  _____

8. Benefits:
- What sort of benefits do you offer students who serve as Peer Leaders (payment, academic credit, reward system, etc.)? _____
  _____

- If academic credit is offered, what type of course, number of credit hours, topics covered, etc.?
  _____
- If financial remuneration is given, how much? _____
- Do you offer any additional "perks"? If so, please explain. _____
  _____

9. Role of the Program Supervisor:
- Who is responsible for supervising your institution's Peer Leader Program? Please list name and title. _____
- List the major duties associated with the supervision of your Peer Leader Program (you may choose to include a copy of a job description)
  1. _____
  2. _____
  3. _____
  4. _____
  5. _____
- Does this individual have any additional support staff? Yes _____ No _____
- If yes, how many? _____

10. Evaluation:
- Is your peer leader program evaluated? Yes _____ No _____
- If yes, by whom (students, peer leaders, instructors, other)? _____
- How do you evaluate your peer leader program (methods)? _____
  _____

- Briefly describe the most recent findings. _____
  _____
  _____
  _____

Waiver Statement: *I understand that the information from this questionnaire will be presented in aggregate with all other responses. However, I do realize that I can permit the presenter(s) to identify my institution by checking the appropriate selection below.*

_____ *Yes, you may identify my institution with the information I am providing.*
_____ *No, present the information in aggregate format only without identifying my institution.*

Signed: _____   Date: _____

About The Authors

John Beck received his Ph.D. from Trinity International University. He currently teaches courses in the language and literature of the Hebrew Bible at Concordia University, Wisconsin. He specializes in the narrative geographical shaping of the Bible. His work can be read in various journals and his recent book, *Translators as Storytellers*. Beck has been the director of the First-Year Experience Program at Concordia since 1989, winning the 1999 Ackman Award for his outstanding contribution to student life. He has been a regular presenter at The First-Year Experience conferences since 1991. In 1999, he was a semifinalist for Outstanding First-Year Advocate, an award sponsored by the National Resource Center for The First-Year Experience and Students in Transition.

John Beck

Gary Brown is Director of the Center for Teaching, Learning, and Technology at Washington State University, where he oversees curriculum and assessment consultation across the WSU campus. He also consults on these subjects throughout the country. He has extensive experience in technology development and has worked to design and implement technology projects across the curriculum. He directs assessment of learning with technology, in the classroom and online, and has overseen a cost-benefit analysis of multiple approaches to technology development and implementation. Brown has written and presented nationally and internationally on assessment, technology, and online instruction. He directs the CTLT Silhouette Project, which hosts Flashlight Online for the Teaching, Learning and Technology Group, an affiliate of the American Association for Higher Education. He has taught English, composition, reader's theatre, program evaluation, and advanced program evaluation. His current research focuses on student learning through

Gary Brown

ferent media. He has bachelor's and master's degrees in English from San Diego State University and an interdisciplinary Ph.D. in English, communication, and education from Washington State University. He is a fellow in the Pew National Learning Community Project.

Marmy Clason

Marmy Clason received her M.A. from Miami University and is pursuing a Ph.D. at Marquette University. She is currently the co-director of the Learning Resource Center at Concordia University, Wisconsin. She also teaches in the Department of Communication and within the First-Year Experience Program. She specializes in gender and communication studies. She has been a contributor at The First-Year Experience Conferences since 1998.

Steven C. Ender

Steven C. Ender has worked in higher education since 1973, serving in a number of teaching and administrative positions. Presently, he is a professor at Indiana University of Pennsylvania and manages the Pennsylvania State System of Higher Education's High School Partnership Programs. During Ender's career, he has planned and implemented learning enhancement programs at three universities, served as a vice president and associate vice president for student affairs, and has taught at both the undergraduate and graduate level. Along with authoring several book chapters and journal articles he has co-written and edited six books in the areas of academic advisement, student affairs contributions to student learning, and training undergraduates to serve as student paraprofessionals in a number of campus roles. His most recent book, *Students Helping Students: A Guide for Peer Educators on College Campuses* (Jossey-Bass, 2000) was co-written with Fred B. Newton.

John N. Gardner

John N. Gardner has led an international movement to enhance the first and senior years on campuses across the country and around the world. He is Senior Fellow of the National Resource Center for The First-Year Experience and Students in Transition and Distinguished Professor Emeritus of Library and Information Science at the University of South Carolina. From 1974 to 1999, Gardner served as Executive Director of the National Resource Center and of the nationally acclaimed University 101 program at USC. He is currently the Executive Director of the Policy Center on the First Year of College, funded by a grant from The Pew Charitable Trusts and based at Brevard College, where he is also Distinguished Professor of Educational Leadership.

Suzanne L. Hamid is Director of First-Year Programs at Lee University in Cleveland, Tennessee. She has also created and continues to oversee one of Lee's most innovative programs, the award-winning Gateway to University Success, a comprehensive strategy that incorporates peer leaders into its first-year experience program. Since 1987, she has held numerous positions in higher education administration, in both student development and academic affairs. More recently, she has focused her professional efforts on peer leadership, with an emphasis on designing curriculum and training materials for institutions desiring to use peer leaders in first-year seminars. She is a frequent workshop presenter on this topic.

Suzanne L. Hamid

Misty Heath is Program Coordinator of New Student Programs at the University of Texas at San Antonio, where she coordinates orientation programs for first-year and transfer students and their families. She also teaches in UTSA's first-year seminar program. She received her M.Ed. in Student Personnel Services from the University of South Carolina, where she worked with the National Resource Center for The First-Year Experience and Students in Transition. She served as a graduate leader for USC's University 101 course, as well as EDLP 520, the course for University 101 peer leaders. Heath graduated magna cum laude from Florida State University and received her B.A. degree in English literature.

Misty Heath

Jean Henscheid is Associate Director of the National Resource Center for The First-Year Experience and Students in Transition, where she directs the production of the Center's monographs, newsletter, journal, and other print resource materials and directs the Center's national research on the first-year and senior year experiences. She has written articles and chapters on first-year seminars, teaching and technology, and peer leadership. Her monograph on senior seminars and capstone courses was published by the Center in 2000. Prior to coming to the Center in 1999, Henscheid directed Washington State University's Freshman Seminar Program, and, as an adjunct assistant professor, coordinated WSU's undergraduate leadership minor and taught undergraduate and graduate courses in research methods and leadership. In the past, she has worked as a newspaper reporter, as an editor for the Westinghouse Corporation, and in enrollment management at Idaho State University.

Jean M. Henscheid

Mary Stuart Hunter

Mary Stuart Hunter, Director of the National Resource Center for The First-Year Experience and Students in Transition, has been with the Center since 1984. During her career, she has advised undecided students, trained faculty and staff academic advisers, and taught USC's first-year seminar, University 101. She is a designer and facilitator of the faculty development workshops of the University 101 Program and hosts a series of annual national and international conferences on The First-Year Experience and other student transitions. She is an adjunct faculty member with USC's College of Education and facilitates workshops at many of the Center's conferences and in other settings on the topic of instructor training and development and peer leader programs. In 1999, the Center published *Solid Foundations: Building Success for First-Year Seminars through Instructor Training and Development*, which Hunter edited.

Keaghan Kay

Keaghan Kay is currently pursuing her doctorate in British literature at the University of South Carolina. In addition to teaching first-year English, she works as an assistant editor at the National Resource Center for The First-Year Experience and Students in Transition. She earned her B.A. in English at the College of the Holy Cross in Worcester, MA and her M.A. in English at Georgetown University in Washington, DC.

Christopher Lynch

Christopher Lynch has been Freshman Seminar Director at Kean University since 1997 and a member of the Department of Communication and Theatre. He has three master's degrees from St. John's University in New York and Princeton Seminary. In 1994, he earned a Ph.D. from Temple University in rhetoric and communication. He has edited two editions of the first-year seminar textbook, *Kean University: Gateway to Your Success*. In 1999, his book *Selling Catholicism: Bishop Sheen and the Power of Television* won the Book of the Year Award from the Religious Communication Association.

Vicky Orazem

Vicky Orazem serves as the coordinator of the General Studies Freshman Seminar course at Montana State University-Bozeman, where she organizes all aspects of course delivery, including coordinating and implementing curriculum design, training instructional staff, and coordinating the peer leader program. She facilitates a section of the freshman seminar and also serves as an academic advisor for "undeclared" students in the General Studies office at Montana State University. She has presented numerous papers and conference sessions, on both the national and international level, on the freshman seminar, the peer leader program, and the assessment of these programs. She holds an M.Ed. and a Ph.D. from the University of Wyoming. Her dissertation examined issues of persistence and retention among undecided students.

Ashley Roller entered Montana State University as an undecided student in her first year. After participating as a student in the General Studies program, she continued as a peer leader. In her senior year, she served as Peer Coordinator for the program. A Presidential Scholar at MSU, Roller received several awards for excellence in leadership, including the Roskie Memorial Scholarship and the Ethel C. Harrison Award. Roller completed a B.S. in exercise science and is currently employed with the American Red Cross. She plans to pursue a master's degree in physical therapy.

Ashley Roller

Jayson VanHook serves as Assistant Director of Admissions at Lee University in Cleveland, Tennessee. As an undergraduate, Jayson was one of four students selected to pilot Lee University's inaugural peer leader program. He is currently pursuing postgraduate studies in organizational/industrial psychology at the University of Tennessee while remaining involved with the work of peer leaders and first-year seminars in the area of assessment.

Jayson VanHook